T0163041

The Book of the Magical Mythical Unicorn

The Book of the Magical Mythical Unicorn

Vakasha Brenman
and Alfonso Colasuonno

BOOKS

Winchester, UK
Washington, USA

JOHN HUNT PUBLISHING

First published by O-Books, 2020
O-Books is an imprint of John Hunt Publishing Ltd., 3 East St., Alresford,
Hampshire SO24 9EE, UK
office@jhpbooks.com
www.johnhuntpublishing.com
www.o-books.com

For distributor details and how to order please visit the 'Ordering' section on our website.

ISBN: 978 1 78904 253 5
Library of Congress Control Number: 2019939548

A CIP catalogue record for this book is available from the British Library.

Design: Stuart Davies

UK: Printed and bound by CPI Group (UK) Ltd, Croydon, CR0 4YY
US: Printed and bound by Thomson-Shore, 7300 West Joy Road, Dexter, MI 48130

We operate a distinctive and ethical publishing philosophy in
all areas of our business, from our global network of authors
to production and worldwide distribution.

Contents

Acknowledgements

The creation of *The Book of the Magical Mythical Unicorn* would not have happened without the gracious support of many individuals. The authors would like to express their deepest gratitude to Michael Mann, Joyce Faust at Art Resource, Ardis Boyd, Katrina Sullivan, Arpita Patel, and our loved ones for their invaluable assistance.

The Authors and Publisher wish to thank all those copyright holders who have given their permission for an extract or illustration to appear. These include the Academy of Sciences in Lisbon, Portugal; Art Resource; Bridgeman-Giraudon; Brill Publishers; the British Museum; Congregation Emanu-El of the City of New York; Benjamin Darling; the International Astronomical Union; Michael Green; HIP; Erich Lessing; the Louvre; the Metropolitan Museum of Art; Musée du Petit Palais; Alfredo Dagli Orti; Paris, Musée de Cluny – Musée national du Moyen Age; the Philosophical Research Society; Larry Brian Radka; RMN-Grand Palais; *Sky & Telescope* magazine; the Trustees of the British Museum; and Michael Urtado. If, however, there are any omissions the authors and publisher will be pleased to correct the matter in any future editions.

Introduction

Wrapped in a cloud came he, by a bright whirlwind borne along. He descended gently from the heavens to the infant fields of Earth, even before the fires of its forming were yet subdued. Thus did the Unicorn possess the brightness of the Light, that he might drive all darkness and obscurity from him. He was called Asallam, of unicorns the firstborn, a creature fearfully wrought and wonderful to behold, bearing a horn of a spiral light.
– Master Magnalucius, *The Codex Unicornis*

Universally, the magical unicorn is the symbol of the spirit. Those who truly see the unicorn are said to be the awakened ones. How did the magical mythical unicorn come into existence and what is its purpose? Why does humanity have such a magnetic pull towards the magical mythical unicorn? English author and spiritual teacher Diana Cooper stated that unicorns "are here to teach you qualities of honour, self-worth, and dignity. Most of all they trigger your innocence, your original divine essence to help you attain the blueprint of who you truly are. Karma melts away in their presence."

No matter who you are or what you believe, the universe abounds with overflowing love for you. There exists an endless amount of possibilities for all of us to reach our full potential. Unfortunately, few have awakened to this truth because of a lack of knowledge, false programming, and past karmic experiences. Our spiritual and psychic gifts are being reawakened by the unicorn. The unicorn serves to remind us of the infinite power that is available to all and the majestic nature of life. The unicorn awakens us from our slumber, offering us the wisdom to become aware of the true nature of reality.

For those who choose to embrace the unicorn into their

lives with the innocence and pure heart of a child, the unicorn will bestow its blessings in a myriad of ways. Unicorns can help people develop in many ways, including bringing forth a person's natural beauty and grace, transmitting a sense of joy and peace, and encouraging transformation through the opening of intuitive gifts. The unicorn truly savors the opportunity to help people transcend the challenges of life in Earth's current third dimension and open themselves to existing in higher vibratory states. It opens our hearts and minds in preparation for both individual and humankind's evolution to higher dimensions for ascension.

The unicorn represents transcendence, spiritual sight, love, and manifestation, though the specific symbolism of the unicorn varies across cultures. As a multidimensional being, the unicorn enters Earth's third dimension when needed or called upon, fulfilling its promise to remain humankind's cherished companion and symbolizing transformation. The unicorn's spiritual sight exposes illusion, revealing the evil nature of separation. The unicorn symbolizes the realization of divine goodness and the higher purpose of life. Through awakening and utilizing your intuitive gifts (or third eye), you can become aware of the unicorn in your life. Once you become aware of the unicorn's presence, you can begin to telepathically communicate with it, and the unicorn can guide you to your destiny. The unicorn offers us a choice: do we stay where we are, trapped in illusion, or do we choose to change and grow? The unicorn helps us to consciously wake up and inspires us to go beyond what we think is possible and embrace what seems impossible. After all, dreams can come true.

The Unicorn: Humankind's Friend Since the Dawn of Time

Before humanity was but a figment in the imagination of the

Great Creator or Universal Mind, so did the unicorn exist. Born out of the void of space and time, and given the name Asallam by the Great Creator as it blessed the unicorn and its horn, the unicorn tarried in the higher dimensions in spiritual bliss. Yet the Universal Mind continued to expand. Likewise, the Universal Mind created our galaxy and our planet, creating the seas that stretch beyond the horizon, the jungles that bustle with life, the mountains that scrape the sky, and all that we cherish.

Into this paradise was humankind born. The stories of the ancients recall this bygone age with the dim memory of a long-forgotten dream. *The Codex Unicornis*, a document written six centuries ago by a mysterious figure named Master Magnalucius who was the founder of a secret society known as the Collegium Gnosticum, reveals their version of the Edenic paradise. There, when humankind was in its infancy, a man and woman existed who delighted in the company of the unicorn, the first of all animals. There, in this utopia, the Great Creator bestowed a special blessing of spiritual sight on the horn of the magical unicorn, a trait which it has retained throughout all the ages.

The blissful state of peace and purest of love that marked the *Codex*'s theory of the Edenic paradise could not be sustained, for there was much growth that humankind must embrace. The nature of one's life is always evolving. Information learned must be absorbed, experienced, and applied effectively. Because of universal truths, the first man and woman could no longer remain in their childhood. They had to descend into third dimension, with all the limitations that this state entails. Though life in third dimension overflows with love, peace, and joy, there are challenges that all must face in their lives. Before the first man and woman entered the third dimension on Earth, the unicorn was presented with a choice by the Great Creator. It could either remain entirely in the higher dimensions, or it could shift between dimensions, enabling the unicorn to continue its loving friendship with humanity. In its commitment to humanity, the unicorn elected to stand by its friends and come into third dimension whenever it was called upon or needed. As author Nancy Hathaway states, "Forever after the unicorn was blessed for its compassion, for it could have stayed in that place of ideal beauty and delight." Ever since, across various cultures and time periods, the unicorn has continued to cross through the dimensions, reminding us of our enduring friendship with this most magical of beasts.

Meeting the Unicorn

The magical mythical unicorn is a transdimensional being, one possessed of the ability to freely travel through the dimensions. When in third dimension on Earth, there are ways of detecting that a unicorn has sojourned in an area. Magical droppings known as periadham have been found in areas where the unicorn has visited. The unicorn's periadham is a crystalline substance in the shape of a sphere. All who have come upon the mystical unicorn's periadham have treasured the substance. There is a longstanding tradition, especially in the British Isles and France, of cairns (piles of stones) marking places where the unicorn has dwelled. These cairns are said to have been erected by those fortunate enough to have either encountered the magical unicorn or have stumbled upon its periadham.

Unicorns are perhaps easiest to engage with while in nature. The unicorn may choose to communicate in a multitude of ways, including telepathically, appearing directly, and sending a physical sign to the earnest seeker. One such way that the magical unicorn often communicates is through revealing a white feather to those who desire its presence. When you find a white feather or see one floating down from the heavens, know that the unicorn is close by and is choosing to reveal itself to you. It has been said that it is best to attempt to communicate with the unicorn before sleep and invite it to bestow its guidance. If asked, the unicorn will surely help you reach the higher dimensions in your dreams, pointing the way to love, peace, healing, and wisdom.

The Universal Unicorn

To the Chinese, it was known as ki-lin. To the Greeks, monokeros. To the Hebrews, re'em. We know this esteemed creature as the unicorn. The unicorn has been present across cultures and faiths throughout the history of civilization. The unicorn has been featured in cave drawings from South America to South Africa, the sculptures of Mesopotamia, the pyramids of Egypt, and the Renaissance art of Europe, among many other artistic works and archaeological sites. The unicorn's lair has been said to have been discovered in North Korea. The unicorn is mentioned in the Old Testament, has been compared to Jesus Christ, was spoken of by Muslim intellectuals, stood as a representative for Vishnu in Hinduism, and served as a symbol for the Buddhist ideal of a quiet, introspective soul with a desire for solitude. These are but a few examples of the unicorn's impact across varied world religions. The many cultures around the globe all have their own unique history with the unicorn, yet one overarching message prevails through all traditions – the unicorn has always remained the friend of humanity.

The Unicorn in India

O Indra, visit us like the thirsty rsya [unicorn] which comes to drink water.
– Rig Veda, 8.4.10

Indian and Hindu Perceptions of the Unicorn

The unicorn, or as it is sometimes called in India, the rsya or eka-shringa, has a rich tradition across the globe, yet few lands have such a deep connection to the magical mythical unicorn as India. The unicorn's presence in India dates back to at least the earliest known civilizations to emerge out of the Indian subcontinent. The unicorn was frequently depicted on seals from Harappa, an early Indian civilization that lasted from 3000–1500 BCE. According to scholar Premendra Priyadarshi, the unicorn was featured on these seals because it was perceived to be a symbol of remarkable power and divinity. In an effort to attract the transcendent energy of the unicorn, many individuals from Harappa and other early Indian civilizations wore a singular horn over their foreheads. This practice was widely observed, including by many brave fighters and kings mentioned in the *Mahabharata,* one of the foremost Hindu scriptures. Scholar Gautama V. Vajracharya believes that the unicorn was not only an animal that was revered by Indians, but that evidence from the *Vedas* (Hindu scriptures) states that the handles of special heated earthen pots of earlier Indian civilizations were partly made from the unicorn's horn.

Throughout the various Indian civilizations, one of the most prominent beliefs about the unicorn was that its horn could counteract poison. There is a prominent legend in India which states that the unicorn would dip its horn in poisoned bodies of water, transforming the waters for the animals who depended on them to drink. This was such a popular myth in India that word of it spread beyond the borders of the Indian subcontinent, including to Europe, where it became known as the water-conning story. One legendary Hindu tale involves the god Siva, who was interestingly given the title of "the one-horned one" in the *Mahabharata* and the *Puranas*. Siva emulated the unicorn's actions by drinking from poisoned waters, and after it quenched his thirst the water lost all power to harm.

1 – Unicorn purifying the water from *Livro de Horas da Condessa de Bertiandos*, a 15th century illuminated book of hours.

India's royalty and aristocracy were vehement believers in the sacredness of the unicorn and its horn. Many Indian kings possessed full horns of the unicorn, valuing them for their mystical and curative qualities, including their ability to eliminate poisons. It has been said that a 13th century Indian king owned a fanciful tricolored cup made entirely of unicorn horn. In time, these types of cups became used not only by kings, but also by nobles, with the most prominent members of Indian society being said to sometimes drink out of unicorn horns. Beliefs expressed in the *Atharvaveda*, a Vedic scripture of Hinduism, led to the unicorn's horn being made into a charm to protect against kshatriya (hereditary disease). In the 16th century, Indian queens regularly wore bracelets made of the bones of the unicorn for their protective attributes. To Indians, the unicorn was not only viewed as a protector, but it also symbolized love, transformation, and a host of other beneficent values. Hindu priests and ascetics have also ascribed the qualities of chastity and solitude to the unicorn, which has served as a model for their lives.

Saved from the Deluge

According to the *Shanti Parva*, one of the books of the *Mahabharata*, long ago, a man named Hiranyaksha was blessed with immortality for his devotion to Brahma, the Creator. Hiranyaksha's newfound immortality led to immense pride, and he began to think of himself as greater than the gods. His ego inflamed, Hiranyaksha sought to persuade humankind to worship him rather than the Hindu deity Vishnu. Hiranyaksha thought himself worthy of praise and hoped to poison the people's minds, spreading lies about how Vishnu was weak and did not truly care for them. However, the people refused to follow Hiranyaksha, remaining steadfast in their worship of Vishnu. In an unquenchable rage brought on by his failure to attract the devotion of humanity, Hiranyaksha became a demon and carried the Earth to the bottom of the cosmic ocean. Despite being wholly submerged, many people adapted and survived. Desperate for help, the survivors faithfully called out in prayer to Vishnu, hoping to be saved from their perilous situation.

Because of the longstanding peace on Earth, Vishnu had been in a deep slumber that spanned several epochs, yet when the people prayed for help, he awakened and reincarnated himself as Varaha, a one-horned beast. Varaha traveled to Hiranyaksha's domain deep below the Earth and fought the demon. For one thousand years, Hiranyaksha attacked Varaha with every conceivable method of combat, yet all were to no effect. To sufficiently humble his opponent, Varaha directed his third eye chakra from his horn at Hiranyaksha. Defeated and humiliated by a greater one than himself, Hiranyaksha finally pleaded for forgiveness. Varaha granted it on the condition that Hiranyaksha be banished from the Earth for eternity. With Hiranyaksha conquered, Varaha lifted the Earth out of the cosmic ocean and set it back into its proper place, earning the praise of his fellow gods and the people.

The story of the great deluge is presented from another perspective in the *Shatapatha Brahmana*. The *Shatapatha Brahmana* tells the story of a man named Manu who was warned by a one-horned fish of a massive flood that was to come. To Hindus, this one-horned fish was an avatar of Vishnu. Vishnu commanded Manu to build a large ship, and later told Manu that when the deluge arrived he would return to save him. Manu, not knowing the one-horned fish was Vishnu, wondered aloud how a small fish could protect him. The one-horned creature explained that when it returned it would be imposing and massive in size, such that no creature of land or sea would dare attack them. Manu followed the one-horned fish's instructions, and when the first signs of the flood had started, he entered his ship. While at sea, the now gigantic one-horned fish returned and swam up to Manu's ship. Vishnu tied the rope of the ship to his horn and then ordered that Manu steer the ship to a tree at the top of a high mountain. Protected from the deluge, Vishnu told Manu that, "I have saved thee. Fasten the ship to a tree; but let not the water cut thee off, whilst thou art on the mountain." Manu once again did as instructed. When the flood started to subside, Manu gradually steered his ship down the mountain, and when he reached the bottom saw that he was alone. Grateful that his life was spared, Manu engaged in worship and austerities, sacrificing into the waters an offering of clarified butter, sour milk, whey, and curds. From these offerings, Vishnu made Manu a female companion. And so it is said that this is how humanity repopulated the Earth.

Genghis Khan and the Unicorn

Perhaps no man has ever been as feared as Genghis Khan. As Emperor of the Mongol people, Khan commanded his army throughout Asia, the Middle East, and Europe, conquering all who opposed him and his formidable troops. In 1224, Genghis Khan led his army to the border of India at Mount Djadanaring in the Himalayas. When they reached the summit, to their amazement the Mongols were met with a unicorn that immediately prostrated itself before Genghis Khan, kneeling three times at his feet. Ssanang Ssetsen, a Mongolian chronicler of the period, reported that after Khan's encounter with the unicorn the fearsome warrior remarked, "This middle kingdom of India before us is the place, men say, in which the sublime Buddha and the Bodhisattvas and many powerful princes of old time were born. What may it mean that this speechless wild animal bows before me like a man? Is it that the spirit of my father would send me a warning out of heaven?" Breathtaken by the appearance, Genghis Khan decided that the unicorn was indeed the reincarnation of his father's spirit warning him against the peril that he would face were he to invade India. Khan ordered his men down the mountain and out of India. They would continue to invade and plunder, though never in the land protected by the unicorn.

When a Man Loves a Unicorn

The *Ramayana* and the *Mahabharata* are the two primary Sanskrit epics of the Hindu religion. In both the *Ramayana* and the *Mahabharata* there exists the story of Rsyasrnga, also known as Ekasrnga in the Buddhist tradition. Rsyasrnga was a boy born of the love between a man and a unicorn.

The story of the half-unicorn, half-human boy begins with a man named Vibhandaka. In his childhood, Vibhandaka's life was little different from most Indian boys; however, while at a parade with his family he saw a holy man. Afterwards, he realized his passion for the spiritual life and desired nothing else but to join this holy man and embark on a life of piety. His family loved him, but they were confused by his overarching desire to join the holy man's ashram, a monastery for Hindu ascetics.

Vibhandaka begged and pleaded for his parents' approval to enter the ashram and serve the holy man, yet his parents refused his request. Not one to be discouraged easily, Vibhandaka persisted in his attempts to persuade his family. Eventually, his parents relented, on one condition. Vibhandaka's mother told her son that if he felt the same way in a year, then he would be allowed to join the holy man at the ashram.

While young boys are prone to momentary whims, the desire to live the life of an ascetic was not a temporal fad for Vibhandaka. After a year had passed, Vibhandaka's parents relented, reluctantly permitting their son to leave their family home and enter the ashram. Once at the sacred place in the forest, Vibhandaka was content to live with the holy man for years. He studied and expanded his knowledge of spiritual truths with his kindly master, although he longed for the love of the family that he had left behind in his pursuit of the sacred. After decades had passed, his master died. With the holy man's other devotees having also passed away by this time, Vibhandaka was now alone at the ashram. Vibhandaka's only companions were the animals that loved him, yet during India's monsoon season even they would disappear and Vibhandaka would become gripped by a profound loneliness. After many years, during the heavy rains of the monsoon season, a magical and gorgeous creature entered Vibhandaka's place of refuge. It was a unicorn with a spiraling horn in the middle of her forehead.

It was love at first sight for Vibhandaka and the unicorn.

Soon after meeting, they were wed; and the Hindu god and goddess of love, along with many other Hindu deities, were said to be among the honored guests at their union. Shortly thereafter, the unicorn gave birth to a child named Rishyashringa. He was a handsome boy, one who appeared human in all respects except for the small horn that grew out of the middle of his forehead. Rishyashringa learned the languages of his parents, both human and unicorn, as well as the languages of all the animals, and was said to be perfect in his ways.

Rishyashringa was loved by his parents, but he would soon have to learn how to make his own way. After many happy years with Vibhandaka, the unicorn died. Vibhandaka was unable to bear living without his partner, passing away almost immediately afterwards. Being left an orphan, Rishyashringa lived a solitary existence in the forest, much as his father did before he fell in love with the beautiful unicorn.

Despite Rishyashringa's solitary lifestyle, he would soon become widely known. Men who wandered in the forest reported tales about the peculiar unicorn boy with the ability to tame all animals, make fire and rain appear at will, and not only restore any plants or fruits which he picked, but make two more grow back for each one that he plucked. During this time, an evil King ruled. A cruel and miserly man who cared little for his subjects, the King's territory was cursed with a famine by Britra, the dragon of drought. The King's advisers were desperate for a solution. They sought to persuade the King to enlist the aid of the magical unicorn boy with incredible powers. The King, being consumed with pride, scoffed at this idea.

The King's country may have been destined to become a wasteland but for the efforts of his daughter Shanta. Not content to allow her father's arrogance to destroy the land, Shanta took the initiative to find Rishyashringa and convince him to help her people. She searched high and low throughout the forest, but was unable to find him. After a while, Shanta stopped by the river to bathe. Rishyashringa was nearby, curious about Shanta, the first woman he had ever seen. He started to secretly follow Shanta through the forest. When Shanta noticed the unicorn boy, she kindly asked him to end the famine in her father's kingdom. Rishyashringa was so enamored with Shanta that the thought of refusing her was absent from his mind. He accepted her request without a second thought and returned with her to the kingdom.

Upon her return, Shanta introduced her father to Rishyashringa. The King could not have been more inhospitable. Despite Shanta's protests, the King demanded that Rishyashringa be taken away. As the King's guards approached, Rishyashringa prayed for rain. Immediately, his prayer was answered. Seeing that Rishyashringa truly had the powers attributed to him, the King begged for mercy from the gods. After three days and nights of nonstop rain, the King's nation was fully restored. Shortly after the rain stopped, the King decided to bestow his blessing on them. Rishyashringa and Shanta married.

Even with an end to his kingdom's drought, a lifetime of pride and miserliness comes with its price. One night, the King fell into a fanciful dream. In his dream, a mighty unicorn galloped towards him. The King attempted to escape, jumping into the abyss below. He grabbed a bush to protect himself from falling and held himself up on a narrow ledge. Directly below the ledge was a dragon breathing flames. Above the ledge was a unicorn. Four serpents suddenly appeared, all rapidly approaching. The King remained gripping the bush, but two mice – one black, one white – began to gnaw at it. The King felt that his demise was imminent. He looked over and saw another ledge, one where a branch dripped with honey. Seeing the honey, the King immediately dismissed all the perils facing him, desperate for a taste. As soon as he was about to move towards the honey-soaked branch, the King remembered the dragon below and woke up in a cold sweat.

Believing that dreams are relevant to waking life, the King demanded that his astrologer, a man named Barlaam, clarify what his dream meant. Barlaam explained the symbolism of each character in this particular dream to the King, "The unicorn is death, which follows us everywhere when it is our turn to meet him. The abyss is the material world into which we fall at birth and from which we cannot escape. The bush represents human life; the mice are day and night, which continually nibble away at the roots of time. The serpents are the four elements of human life. The dragon represents hell. And the honey is the sweetness of surrender which we must know before we can die peaceably." The King was petrified by the answer that he had received. He asked Barlaam if the dream signified that his death was imminent. In response, Barlaam remarked, "Arrange your affairs. When the dream comes again, open your mouth and let the honey drip upon your tongue."

Obstinate by nature, the King refused to embrace his fate. The King avoided sleep for two days until his body could no longer tolerate the deprivation. When he finally fell asleep, the King entered the same dream. He tasted the sweet honey, never returning to the waking world. After the King's death, the kingdom flourished under the new rulership of Shanta and Rishyashringa.

The Unicorn in China

The deer untethered roams the wild where it wishes in search of food. Seeing this liberty, wise man, fare solit'ry as the Unicorn, free everywhere and at odds with none, content with what comes your way, enduring peril without alarm. Fare solit'ry as the Unicorn, like a lion fearless of the howling pack, like the breeze ne'er trapped in a snare, like the lotus unsoiled by its stagnant pool. Fare solit'ry as the Unicorn.

– Excerpt from a Buddhist hymn

The Ki-Lin

The unicorn, known to the Chinese people as the ki-lin, has had a monumental role in Chinese culture and civilization. The traditional Chinese creation myth states that the universe began in chaos. From this formless state, Pangu, the first living being and creator figure in Chinese mythology, started to create the worlds. The ki-lin, along with China's three other auspicious creatures (the phoenix, the tortoise, and the dragon), helped Pangu chip away at the light, the dark, and the five elements. After eighteen thousand years of diligent labor, they all witnessed the breathtaking beauty of the universe that had been created. With the task of creation completed, each of the four auspicious animals sought a territory in which to abide. The ki-lin chose the lush forests of China.

From the beginning of creation to the present day, the mythical ki-lin has been an important part of Chinese culture. A ki-lin revealed the symbols of the Chinese language to Fu Hsi, China's first emperor. A ki-lin foretold the birth and death of Confucius, one of China's greatest wisdom teachers and the creator of the *I Ching*, an oracular book that forms the foundations of Confucianism and Taoism and is described by translator Richard Wilhelm as "unquestionably one of the most important books in the world's literature." Whenever a ki-lin appeared, the people rejoiced at their elusive visitor from the higher dimensions. They knew that when a ki-lin appeared in China, it meant that either a magnanimous leader was to be born, die, or that the government was ruling with its citizens' best interests in mind. When a ki-lin was seen, magical occurrences were never far behind.

The Chinese people believe that the sacred ki-lin possesses virtues that exemplify the highest ideals of their culture, including knowing good from evil, being reverential to one's parents, and piously regarding one's ancestors. Ki-lins exceed even the pinnacle of humanity in their character, as their actions extend far beyond the basics of an ethical life. It has been relayed that ki-lins cannot lie or deceive, and they are believed to be so benevolent that they are sensitive even to the plight of a trampled blade of grass. They do not possess quarrelsome natures and refuse to fight. Individuals fortunate enough to have encountered a ki-lin have been dazzled by their sweet voices.

Since ancient times, ki-lins have been esteemed by the Chinese as the pinnacle of the animal kingdom. In conjunction with the dragon, the phoenix, and the tortoise, the ki-lin has been honored as one of China's four auspicious creatures. These auspicious animals are known to have a variety of supernatural powers, including the ability to ward off evil spirits. Ki-lins are sometimes thought to reside in the palace of Huang Ti, also known as the Yellow Emperor, who after his reign in the 27th century BCE became one of China's foremost deities.

How the Chinese Language was Invented

Emperor Fu Hsi reigned in China from 2852 to 2737 BCE and was beloved for his generous heart and effective leadership.

During his reign, the Emperor introduced fishing, hunting, and the domestication of animals, all new ways for his people to better feed themselves. Emperor Fu Hsi also provided for his people's spirituality by introducing them to the foundations of consciousness and universal spiritual principles through the trigrams, which are symbols that would later be used for divination in the *I Ching*. Despite the major advances that the Emperor brought to his people, he still felt that they needed a better way to communicate. The Emperor called upon his advisers and the brightest minds of his kingdom for solutions, but it was to no avail. He called upon his own creative gifts, but no ideas were forthcoming. Though Fu Hsi governed with kindness, he did so with great sadness and a heavy heart, as day after day passed without any solution to solve this communication problem.

One morning, Fu Hsi awakened with a start. The despondency that had overwhelmed him was replaced with boundless energy. The Emperor had an intuition that the answer to his problem would be revealed in his favorite place of quiet contemplation, along the banks of the Yellow River. And so the Emperor left his palace for the first time in weeks, traveling with his guards to the river. Once he arrived, Fu Hsi dismissed his men and sat by the banks. The river rushed and rippled, the birds chirped and fluttered, the willow trees cast their dewy scent all throughout, yet Fu Hsi's dark mood returned even amidst the wonders of creation.

The Emperor patiently waited by the river, questioning whether this endeavor was futile, but hoping that his premonition would still be realized. Suddenly, the ki-lin appeared before this wise and noble ruler. He was mystified as to why the sacred ki-lin had chosen to appear before him. Instantly, the Emperor bowed before the noble creature, not thinking himself worthy of this occurrence. The ki-lin reassured Fu Hsi that he was indeed worthy, and that it was responding to the Emperor's earnest desire to help his people communicate better. Before Fu Hsi's eyes, the characters that were to become the Chinese language started to magically form on the ki-lin's body. Fu Hsi stared at the symbols in amazement, almost mesmerized, until he was startled out of his reverie by the gentle laugh of the ki-lin. At the banks of the Yellow River, the ki-lin not only showed him, but taught Fu Hsi the symbols that would become the Chinese language. Once Fu Hsi comprehended the written symbols, the ki-lin returned to the higher realms. Fu Hsi watched in amazement as the ki-lin dematerialized before his eyes. The Emperor immediately caught up with his guards and they hurried back to his court, where he presented and taught the ki-lin's magical gift of the Chinese language to his people.

The Ki-Lin's Reappearance

Emperor Huang Ti, who reigned from 2698 to 2598 BCE, was one of China's most exalted leaders, revered by his people as a just and intelligent ruler, and deified as the Yellow Emperor. Throughout his entire life, he had devoted himself to working diligently to provide for his people's basic needs. Seeing that a semi-nomadic lifestyle based on hunting and gathering was not adequate for his people's well-being, Huang Ti built China's first towns, its first structures able to withstand the elements, and helped China become prosperous through trade.

In his youth and middle age, Huang Ti had a vigorous disposition, yet in his twilight years the Emperor had begun to retire from his duties because of his declining health. Huang Ti groomed the next generation of leaders to provide for the needs of his people, but spent most of his days outside the palace, fondly remembering his younger years. As Huang Ti sat outside the palace one morning, wrapped in his memories, the interdimensional ki-lin appeared to him.

Huang Ti instantly recognized the creature and felt humbled that the divine ki-lin had chosen to present itself to him. Almost as soon as it appeared, the ki-lin disappeared, yet the Emperor wasn't forlorn. He realized that the mythic ki-lin had come to him to acknowledge the record of good deeds that marked his life. Within a matter of days, Huang Ti died. Legend says that there was a deep smile on his face when he passed away, and some say he went into the next life on the back of a magical ki-lin. Such was the happy fate for the Emperor who made it his life's mission to help and serve.

The Birth and Death of a Great Sage

One morning, in despair over many years of unsuccessfully trying to conceive a child, a woman named Ching-tsae went searching for the legendary holy temple hidden deep in the forests of the kingdom of Lu. She had ventured there with her mother as a young girl and fondly remembered performing her devotions at the temple that seemed to soar to the skies. Knowing that it would be difficult to locate the temple, Ching-tsae set out as the final rays of moonlight were beginning to give way to the sun rising over the horizon. With the emerging sunlight guiding her way, she found the right path through the dense forest to the temple. Once Ching-tsae rediscovered the temple, she performed her devotions, and then started to meditate.

Ching-tsae emptied her mind of all the hopes and fears of daily life and sunk deep into a meditative state. While in the peaceful bliss of meditation she received a supernatural vision. Five mystical entities stood near the temple's altar. Perched on top of the altar was a ki-lin. These entities, appearing as beings, explained to Ching-tsae that they were the embodiments of the planetary spirits. Ching-tsae inquired as to their purpose. The spirits remained silent. Out of the magical ki-lin's mouth came a chunk of jade with the inscription, "The son of the essence of water shall succeed to the withering Chou [Dynasty] and he will become a throneless king." The ki-lin tilted its head in the direction of the jade, its spiraled horn pointing straight at the majestic stone. Despite Ching-tsae's hesitation, the ki-lin did not move an inch until she picked up the object. Not wishing to take the ki-lin's magical gift without giving something in return, Ching-tsae untied the ribbon from her luxuriously flowing hair and securely fastened it to the ki-lin's horn with warmth in her heart and a smile on her face.

Ching-tsae returned to her home that evening. With a jubilant energy radiating from her essence, she showed her kindly husband Heih the exquisite piece of jade, then relayed the wonderment of the amazing events that had transpired at the temple. While neither Ching-tsae nor her husband understood the meaning of the encounter with the ki-lin and the five planetary spirits, they did agree that what happened was a fortuitous event. Ching-tsae and Heih were both aware of the legend that a mythical ki-lin appeared either upon the birth or death of exceptional leaders and speculated that the ki-lin's jade was an omen of such an event.

Ching-tsae kept the treasured piece of jade by her bedside. She had heard stories since the earliest days of her childhood that jade was a prophetic stone. Transfixed by its beauty, she gazed into the magnificent jewel every night, pondering as to how the ki-lin's prophecy would unfold. One evening, Ching-tsae experienced a completely unexpected event – the ki-lin's jade started to vibrate. Before her eyes, the jade expanded and contracted, and suddenly shattered into five pieces, each piece representing the five sacred planetary spirits. Ching-tsae was bewildered by the shattering of the ki-lin's treasured gift and pondered the meaning of this occurrence. Heih tried to offer comforting words to his wife, but it was to no avail. Even the exhaustion of a sleepless night could not soothe Ching-tsae's overwhelming anxiety and confusion. Right before the first rays of morning sunlight peeked out of the darkness, Ching-tsae heard the melodic voice of the transcendent ki-lin as it began to telepathically communicate with her. *The jade was an omen. Do not be remorseful. Be joyful, for you are to birth a great leader. By his mind and heart, he will touch many lives.* The mystical ki-lin's message immediately comforted Ching-tsae. She relaxed into a deep sleep. Nine months later, she gave birth to a son. Ching-tsae and Heih named him Confucius.

As foretold by the ki-lin, Confucius would become a prominent leader, transforming China into a more just and kind land through his teachings. Revealed in the jade, Confucius received the spiritual knowledge that would define his philosophy, later called Confucianism. According to legend and presented by the Falun Dafa organization, Confucius explained, "Jade is precious not because it is rarer, but because the quality of jade corresponds to a gentleman's virtue. It corresponds to such virtues as benevolence, wisdom, righteousness, propriety, loyalty, and trustworthiness, and it also corresponds to the ways of the heaven and earth." Jade is a symbol of the unicorn.

A few weeks before Confucius' death, an assembly of hunters led by the Duke of Lu happened upon the same temple where the ki-lin and the planetary spirits had appeared to Ching-tsae. Unlike Confucius' mother, the Duke's warlike men were not spiritually oriented. When in private, they would regularly whisper amongst themselves about the folly of the Duke's reverence for Confucius and his teachings. Not able to comprehend Confucius' magnificent wisdom, they thought the Duke a simple-minded fool for regularly turning to Confucius for guidance.

When the Duke and his men entered the temple, the ki-lin was again perched on the altar. The ki-lin calmly observed the men, who laughed and insulted the creature, unaware of the ki-lin's sacred nature. The Duke, so enchanted by the beauty of the ki-lin, did not think to order his men not to attack. One of the Duke's men, encouraged by his companions, stabbed the ki-lin with his sword. The Duke immediately ran in front of the wounded ki-lin to prevent any further injury, then ordered his men to carry the ki-lin back to town. The Duke's men complied, yet their eyes revealed the cruelty in their hearts.

Distraught over the attack and eager for advice, the Duke of Lu conveyed what had occurred to Confucius and requested that his spiritual teacher visit the wounded ki-lin. Confucius agreed to the Duke's request because he desired to see the magnificent ki-lin. The Duke led Confucius to an enclosed area outside of his property. Although he had been guided by the ki-lin his entire life, Confucius was overcome with joy as he beheld the physical essence of the ki-lin. He gazed at the ribbon on the ki-lin's horn and remembered the stories that his mother used to tell him of her encounter with the prophetic ki-lin. He knew that the ribbon on this ki-lin's horn was the same ribbon as the one mentioned in her astonishing stories. The Duke anxiously asked Confucius if he knew of the significance of the ki-lin's appearance at the temple. Confucius remarked that it was yet to be seen what the appearance of the ki-lin meant, though inwardly he smiled and knew it was there to escort him to the next dimension. After looking into the soulful eyes of the enclosed ki-lin, Confucius told the Duke that the creature should be freed. The Duke concurred. Once the ki-lin was released from the enclosure, it ventured towards the forest, turning around to smile at Confucius and leaving a chunk of jade before it hurried off.

After his magical encounter with the ki-lin, Confucius stopped writing. Within a matter of weeks, he passed away, returning to the source. It is said that before he died, the multidimensional ki-lin ushered Confucius into the next world, a reward for his exceptional benevolence and compassion for all.

The Appearance to Wu Ti

Emperor Wu Ti was an esteemed leader who ruled the Han Dynasty during the 2nd and 1st centuries BCE. One night, while the Emperor was still a young man, Wu Ti spotted a ki-lin on the edge of his palace's grounds. Instantly, the Emperor's heart filled with delight, as legend told that the appearance of a ki-lin was a positive omen, one that signaled that a leader was ruling justly. Wu Ti approached the ki-lin, only to watch the elusive creature vanish before his eyes. Afterwards, the Emperor told everyone about his encounter with the ki-lin. Remembering the magical sensation of seeing the ki-lin, the light of pure love shined from his eyes every time he regaled his companions with the marvelous story.

Wu Ti's insatiable desire to once again physically attract another visit from the ki-lin became the driving obsession in his life. As the Emperor's youth faded into middle age, he ordered a magnificent pagoda built to honor the mythic ki-lin, hoping that the structure would attract another visit in the earthly plane. Unfortunately, Wu Ti's action was to no avail. In an otherwise exceptional life, one in which he gave and received so voluminously, the Emperor's one regret upon his deathbed was that he was not able to catch a second glimpse of the mysterious ki-lin.

The False Ki-Lin

Emperor Yung Loh of the Ming dynasty, which reigned in China from 1368 to 1644, was a well-respected leader who sought to establish trade with peoples across the globe. One such voyage that Yung Loh commissioned in this pursuit of trading partners and new alliances was a journey to the eastern coast of Africa.

When the sailors arrived, they made the acquaintance of the local people, and although communication was difficult because of language barriers, mutually advantageous trade was soon established. Afterwards, as was the local custom, the sailors' new African friends presented them with a gift – a clumsy, 18-foot tall giraffe. When the chief of the village pointed to the animal and exclaimed, "Girin," the sailors were awestruck. They wondered if this could this really be a revered ki-lin.

The sailors returned to China with their gift. With great reverence and ceremony, they presented the girin to the Emperor. Being a man of good humor, Yung Loh was amused at his men's honest mistake of perceiving the giraffe as a ki-lin and received the gift gracefully. The Emperor exhibited the giraffe at his palace, even going so far as to proclaim it a ki-lin, though Yung Loh knew that the magical mythical ki-lin was an entirely different creature from the animal that his men brought him.

The Ki-Lin in Contemporary China

To the Chinese people, the ki-lin symbolizes all the transformative building blocks of a wonderful life, including love, happiness, health, and prosperity. The ki-lin does not only bring forth good fortune, but also helps prevent evil from encroaching. Outside of many Chinese homes are stones with carved depictions of the ki-lin. These stones with the magical ki-lin's image on them are believed to prevent harmful demons from entering a household.

The ki-lin is a major part of festive celebrations in China. The popular Mid-Autumn Festival has both children and adults engaging in a lively and joyous dance that is said to mimic the trot of the ki-lin. On wedding days, many brides make sure to sit on chairs affixed with the image of the ki-lin, believing that doing so will help them conceive wise leaders and virtuous children. The ki-lin, being embedded in the psyche of the Chinese for millennia, continues to remain an extremely vital part of both contemporary Chinese mythology and daily life.

The Unicorn in East Asia

A wise man never plays leapfrog with a unicorn.
– Tibetan proverb

The Unicorn in Japan

The Japanese have a longstanding tradition with the magical mythical unicorn. In Japan, two distinct types of unicorns are honored. One is the ki-rin, which shares the same qualities as China's ki-lin. The ki-rin is peaceful, benevolent, holy, and extremely elusive. The other type of unicorn revered by the Japanese is the sin-you. Tradition states that the sin-you looks like a lion, except for its large spiraled horn. The Japanese believed that the sin-you protected people from danger through its ability to determine whether those accused of crimes were innocent or guilty. In ancient Japan, violent lawbreakers knew that seeing the sin-you in court was an ominous sign for them.

The Unicorn in Vietnam

In Vietnam, the unicorn is known as the ky-lan or ly, and its tradition dates back for millennia. Stories tracing back 2,700 years to the Duong dynasty have connected the ky-lan to peace, prosperity, happiness, longevity, righteousness, good luck, and intelligence. The Vietnamese consider the ky-lan to be one of their four sacred creatures, along with the dragon, the phoenix, and the tortoise. According to the Vietnamese Student Association of North Carolina State University, the ky-lan has the body of an antelope, the hooves of a horse, the tail of a buffalo, and a single horn. The ky-lan is perhaps currently best known for the energetic unicorn dance that serves to mark the celebration of the lunar new year at Vietnam's Têt festival.

The Unicorn in Korea

In 2012, evidence of the unicorn's existence emerged out of North Korea. A rock engraved with the words Unicorn's Lair was discovered by archaeologists inside a cave near the city of Pyongyang. The Unicorn's Lair is thought to be the pyramid tomb burial site for the unicorn of Dongmyeong of Goguryeo, a king who reigned from 37 to 19 BCE and a descendent of the grandson of China's Yellow Emperor.

The Unicorn in Mongolia

The Mongolian unicorn is known as the poh. The poh resembles a horse, with a white body, black tail, teeth and claws like a tiger, a howl like the roll of a drum, and a single horn. The poh is believed to have been helpful to the Mongol army, where it served as an indomitable warrior. Perhaps the Mongolian tradition of the poh led Genghis Khan to avoid invading India when the unicorn approached him and his army at Mount Djadanaring.

The Unicorn in Tibet

In Tibet, the unicorn is known as the tso'po. Tibetans believe that the tso'po travels in herds throughout Tibet and the lands of the Tatar people of Xinjiang, their northern neighbors. There is an extensive tradition within Tibet of utilizing the horn of the tso'po for a variety of magical and ritual purposes.

The Unicorn Appears in Nepal to Maya, the Buddha's Mother

In the 6th century BCE, King Suddhodana of the mighty Satya tribe of Nepal married Maha Maya, Princess of the Koliya tribe. On a night illuminated by a bright full moon, shortly after their being joined together, Maya had a dream. In her dream, she could feel four spirits taking her to Lake Anotatta in the densely wooded part of the Himalayan mountain range. First, the spirits bathed Maya in the lake, then they decked her out in the finest clothes, perfumes, and flowers. Afterwards, a white unicorn appeared before Maya, encircling her three times before its spirit entered her womb. When she awoke, Maya was puzzled by the meaning of her dream, but understood that it had a deep profundity. She awakened her husband, relayed the dream to him, and asked him for his interpretation on its significance. Suddhodana was unsure, and so he called on his wise men to interpret his wife's dream. The wise men announced that Maya had been chosen to birth an exceptional son, one whose teachings would inspire and enlighten humanity throughout the ages. Both Suddhodana and Maya were extremely happy when they heard the news, inviting all in their kingdom to a grand feast to celebrate the forthcoming arrival of Maya's child, who would later become the Buddha, the wise and noble Siddhartha Gautama.

The Unicorn in Siberia

The Siberian unicorn (Elasmotherium sibiricum) has long been incorrectly assumed to have gone extinct around 350,000 years ago, yet new evidence from Andrey Shpanski, a paleontologist at Russia's Tomsk State University, contradicts this false assumption. Shpanski performed radiocarbon AMS-method analysis on a unicorn skull recovered in the village of Kozhamzhar in Kazakhstan and found that this fossil dated to around 27,000 BCE. Furthermore, the recovery of this unicorn's skull in Kazakhstan indicates that the unicorn's habitat extended far beyond the frozen tundra of Siberia into the steppes of Central Asia and quite possibly beyond.

The Unicorn in the Middle East

Wherever they may have come from, and wherever they may have gone, unicorns live inside the true believer's heart. Which means that as long as we can dream, there will be unicorns.
– Bruce Coville, "The Lore of the Unicorn"

The Karkadann

In much of the Middle East region, the unicorn is known as the karkadann. The karkadann has been a part of many of humankind's earliest civilizations and its presence is extensive in ancient Middle Eastern civilizations, including the Sumerians, Assyrians, and Babylonians. The karkadann was mentioned in the Babylonian Code of Hammurabi, the first set of codified laws in human history, and in the Sumerian Epic of Gilgamesh, one of humanity's earliest surviving creative works.

It is said that on the karkadann's forehead is a black spiraled horn that was commented on by Al-Damiri, a 14th century Islamic writer of natural history. Like other varieties of unicorn, the karkadann has a love of solitude; and is known to be fond of wandering alone in deserted places. The karkadann's natural habitat are the deserts of India and Persia, though some claim that its domain extended as far as northeastern Africa.

Legends About the Karkadann

According to legend, the karkadann had a profound friendship with the ring dove. When a ring dove spotted a karkadann, the bird would land on the karkadann's horn. In exchange for her friendship, the karkadann would guard the ring dove's nest. While under the karkadann's protective watch, the ring dove was known to entertain it with melodic songs.

To the Arabic people, the karkadann is celebrated for its dowsing abilities, using its magical horn to uncover water. In the harsh desert regions of the Middle East, this trait proved admirable. For Bedouins and others on long desert journeys, the sighting of a karkadann was quite favorable. In present-day Iraq, there are a variety of Islamic prayer beads known as tears of the karkadann. An accompanying legend tells of the karkadann wandering all day throughout the desert, and when it finally finds water it weeps in delight. As its tears fall into the water, they become holy reddish beads.

Many powerful attributes have been ascribed to the karkadann's horn. Throughout the region, there are common beliefs that the karkadann's horn can protect against the evil eye and black magick, prevent accidents from occurring, cure colic, epilepsy, and other diseases, and act as a charm against attacks from scorpions. Popular folklore in the Middle East, Persia, and North Africa states that the karkadann's horn could be shaped into a magical flute or ground up into a powder and used as an antidote for all poisons. Despite these legends, there had never been a widespread desire to acquire the horn of the karkadann amongst the Arabs, for the karkadann and its horn were treated with reverence, rather than as mere commodities.

Jibra'il ibn Bakhtishu' ibn Jurjis was a 9th century Assyrian physician who composed a bestiary known as the *Kitab Na't Al-Hayawan* that became widely read within the Middle East. Ibn Bakhtishu's bestiary included the karkadann. The *Na't* states that the karkadann's native habitat was in the lands of Nubia and Abyssinia (Ethiopia) in Africa. According to the *Na't*, if the karkadann's horn is heated it can protect people against harmful magic spells and can also be worn as a necklace to protect people from evil.

The *Na't* includes the universal myth of the water-conning story. The *Na't* states that in the Shahrus desert of the

Oriental region, "throughout the whole length and breadth of this desert, there is no watercourse or place with water in it, except for one pool into which these rivers flow when they contain water. There the water collects, but when it has done so it becomes a deadly poison, and any animal that drinks it dies immediately. So the animals in that desert avoid it and do not drink it at all. They continue in this manner until, thirst-stricken, they are at the point of death, with no escape from that desert and nowhere in it where they may seek water. Then they all gather around this animal and beseech it submissively and humbly in order to appeal to it. In this appeal are united all the carnivores and herbivores, which are naturally hostile to one another. When it sees them acting thus it responds and proceeds to lead them like their Prince with them as followers... and when it reaches that pool it bathes in it and bathes its horns repeatedly in its water. Then it begins to drink the water, and after that the wild beasts and predatory animals go down to the water and drink and bathe in that poisonous pool, the water of which has become fresh and good. It remains sweet and good for thirty nights, and then it reverts to its previous state, so they avoid it. Then, they go back to the dabba [karkadann] to beseech it to do the same again. Things continue in the way we have described until winter comes and there is abundant water."

Adorned with a Horn

Until the 19th century, many women of Syria, Lebanon, and Israel wore a special article of clothing called a tantour. The tantour was an artificial horn resembling that of a karkadann's horn that was placed over women's foreheads. It was most commonly worn by members of the Maronite sect of Christianity and by the reclusive Druze people, who practice a faith which blends elements of Islam, Christianity, Judaism, Hinduism, and Gnosticism. Women would receive the tantour upon their wedding day as a gift from their husbands, and it was perceived as a signal of rank. Oftentimes, the tantour was adorned with gems and pearls. Many tantours were elongated, with some measuring thirty inches. Although the tantour was a splendid sight, it was rare to behold one in public, as they were hidden from view by the mandil, a headcovering worn over the tantour.

2 – Illustration of the tantour from Larry Brian Radka's *Historical Evidence for Unicorns.*

The Biblical Re'em

The Tanakh is one of the primary religious texts of the Jewish faith. Within the Tanakh, there are various references to a mysterious animal known as the re'em. The Septuagint, a group of seventy-two scholars tasked with translating the scriptures from Hebrew to Greek in the 3rd and 2nd centuries BCE, translated the word re'em as monokeros (one-horned), believing it to be the unicorn. The Septuagint's translation of re'em as unicorn has had a major influence on generations of followers of Judaism.

The re'em, i.e. unicorn, is mentioned nine times in the Tanakh: in Numbers (23:22 and 24:8), in Deuteronomy (33:17), in Job (39:9–12), in Psalms (22:21; 29:6; and 92:10), in Isaiah (34:7), and in Daniel (8:5). In both references in Numbers, the unicorn is portrayed as having strength equal to the Lord. In Deuteronomy, the power of the Hebrew God Yahweh is compared to the power of the unicorn's horn. This passage has also been perceived by some as a reference to the unicorn's ability to successfully combat evil. In the Book of Job, Yahweh struggles to enlighten Job, a pious man who has endured much worldly misfortune despite his prideful declarations of devotion to the Lord. In chapter 39, Yahweh reproaches Job for his hubris. Yahweh instructs Job by asking him a series of rhetorical questions, including whether the unicorn would be willing to serve and submit to him instead of serving the Lord. Utilizing the ideal of the all-knowing unicorn as a teaching device, Yahweh guides Job out of his despondency and helps him realize that he should try to understand and not attempt to control every outcome in life. In chapter 22:21 of the Book of Psalms, King David asks Yahweh to, "Save me from the lion's mouth, even as thou hast heard me from the horn of the unicorn." In chapter 29:6 of the Book of Psalms, the omnipotence of Yahweh is referenced by stating that He can make a mountain leap like a unicorn. The last mention within the Book of Psalms is in chapter 92:10, which states, "But my horn shalt thou exalt like the horn of a unicorn: I shall be anointed with fresh oil." In the Book of Isaiah, the unicorn serves as an avenger for the Lord, bestowing retribution against evil individuals. The Book of Daniel's reference to the unicorn differs markedly from the unicorn's other mentions in the Tanakh, as the unicorn in this passage is often thought by Jewish scholars to symbolize Alexander the Great in a prophecy of the rise and fall of Alexander's Macedonian Greek empire. Though each reference to the unicorn is different in manner of presentation, the Tanakh consistently describes the unicorn as a holy and powerful animal.

The unicorn, in addition to its specific references in the Tanakh, has long been associated within Judaism with the twelve tribes of Israel. Manasseh, the grandson of Jacob and son of Joseph, is represented within the Judaic tradition by the unicorn, whereas his twin brother Ephraim is represented by the bull.

3 – Gold engraving of a unicorn, representing Manasseh, and bull, representing Ephraim, on the door of Congregation Emanu-El of the City of New York.

This symbolism of the unicorn and the bull to reference Manasseh and Ephraim is widespread within Judaism, and artistic portrayals of the unicorn and bull have appeared on doors, artworks, and tapestries associated with synagogues throughout the world. Fascinatingly, sometimes the bull is replaced by a lion in these depictions. One such example is in a work of art from the 1600s in the town of Hodorov in Poland, which has an artistic representation of a lion and a unicorn on the ceiling of a synagogue.

David and the Unicorn

Many of the psalms in the Book of Psalms are attributed to King David, including Psalm 22. In Psalm 22, King David asked the Lord to, "Save me from the lion's mouth, even as thou hast heard me from the horn of the unicorn." Though there is no additional context provided in this psalm or in other sections of the Tanakh to explain the event to which King David is referring, the Talmud explains it in greater detail.

According to a Talmudic story in *Midrash Tillin Terumah*, fol. 21B, "Once while keeping his flock in the wilderness David climbed upon the back of a sleeping unicorn which he mistook for a mountain, thinking that by so doing he would be better able to watch his scattered flock. All of a sudden the unicorn awoke and stood erect, and David was thus perched so high that he reached heaven. Then cried he unto God and said, 'If thou wilt bring me down in safety from this unicorn I will build for thee a temple of a hundred cubits, like the horn of this unicorn.' Some say that the measure refers to the *length*, and others say that it refers to the *width* (diameter) of the horn. What did the Holy One – blessed be He! – do? He conjured a lion to appear, which so frightened the unicorn that it crouched down before him as before a King, and thus David was able to dismount, but as soon as he caught sight of the lion he was alarmed, and therefore it is said, (Psalm 22:21) 'Save me from the lion's mouth, even as thou hast heard me from the horn of the unicorn.'" This Talmudic passage serves as an example of the awesome power that the Jewish people ascribed to the unicorn.

The Unicorn in Persia

Dreams are the playground of unicorns.
– Author Unknown

The Unicorn in Zoroastrianism

Zoroastrianism is a monotheistic religion founded in Persia (present day Iran) around the 2nd millennium BCE. The Zoroastrian faith is currently practiced by approximately 2.6 million people, its followers mostly concentrated in Iran and India. Founded by the prophet Zoroaster (also known as Zarathustra), Zoroastrianism places responsibility on the individual to choose their path in life. One of the central questions the Zoroastrian faith asks of its adherents is whether a person will choose to embrace the good of creator Ahura Mazda and his spirit, known as Spenta Mainyu, or the evil of Ahriman and his spirit Angra Mainyu.

The Zoroastrian Bundahishn (holy scripture) was written around the 7th century CE, but the ideas it focused on had been in existence for at least a thousand years. The unicorn, known as the korseck in Iran, has a significant role within the Zoroastrian scriptures. In the Bundahishn, the korseck is worshipped as a sacred beast and said to symbolize both the role of Ahura Mazda and the raw power through which Ahriman is to be conquered. According to journalist Rüdiger Robert Beer in his book *Unicorn: Myth and Reality*, when the Zoroastrian korseck "urinates into the waters they become purified." Much like other variations of the global water-conning story, the Zoroastrians have a comparable tradition in which the korseck purifies water. Though distinct in culture and faith, these universal legends all point to the unicorn's desire to be of service to others and its enduring association with purity and regeneration.

Iskandar and His Unicorn

History records few individuals of such magnitude as Alexander the Great of the 4th century BCE. Alexander, known in Persia as Iskandar, set out from his Macedonian home and created an empire that stretched from Greece to the edge of India all before he reached the age of thirty-three. How could a young man have performed such a feat?

When Iskandar was thirteen, his father Philip received a present from a group of noblemen – a magical unicorn. Philip was unable to mount his gift, so he decided to offer the unicorn as a companion to any individual able to ride it. While many tried, all failed, yet Philip's own son Iskandar sought to take on this daunting challenge. Much to his father's surprise, Iskandar succeeded. Whereas Iskandar's father and the others had tried to subdue the unicorn through brute

4 – *How Alexander the Great Mounted Bucephalus, a miniature from Histoire du Grand Alexandre* by Jean Vauquelin, 1460.

force, Iskandar spoke gentle words, offered it delicious food, and only then attempted to mount it. The unicorn placed its magnificent spiraled horn over Iskandar's heart and, intuiting that Iskandar's intentions were pure, offered no resistance to its new friend.

Iskandar's unicorn, which he named Bucephalus, accompanied him on his adventures. It is said that Bucephalus was the key to Iskandar's successful battles against a variety of mythical foes, including: the dog-headed men, the giant women with horned helmets, the Cyclops, the wild hairy men, the fire-breathing birds, the wild elephants and wild men of Arbela, and the deceiving divs. In Persia, the divs have traditionally been perceived as false gods, supernatural beings with evil intentions and ostensibly limitless power. Perhaps no battle of Iskandar's is more celebrated within Persian folklore than the one he fought against the divs.

After having traveled an immense distance for a single day, a group of beautiful women appeared to Iskandar and his army as they were about to set up camp for the night. Iskandar's men, having been without companionship for a long period while in their leader's service, became intrigued by this seemingly fortuitous occurrence; however, Iskandar suspected that these women's appearance was nothing but an illusion. Iskandar refused to match their gaze and called on his men to resist their charms. Enraged by Iskandar's action, the divs shapeshifted into their hideous true forms. With much help from Bucephalus, Iskandar and his men conquered the divs in battle.

After a lifetime of victorious actions, Iskandar succumbed to the temptation of believing that he was omnipotent. One day, in a bout of audacity, Iskandar announced to his men that he could fly. While unable to openly doubt Iskandar's claim, his men whispered amongst themselves that Iskandar had gone mad. With the help of Bucephalus, Iskandar enlisted the efforts of two griffins to assist him in this wondrous endeavor. The griffin is an animal that is part lion and part eagle, blessed with the ferocity of the lion, and the agility and flying ability of the eagle. The griffins held Iskandar and Bucephalus up, one on each side of the pair. On Iskandar's command, the griffins began to fly them up to the heavens. At a certain distance, Iskandar heard a commanding voice from above that ordered him to turn back. Despite the efforts of Bucephalus and the griffins, there was no way for Iskandar to pass any further. He had reached a place no mortal man was permitted to traverse.

The Unicorn in Ancient Greece and Rome

*The filings of this [unicorn] horn, if given in a potion, are
an antidote to poisonous drugs... These horns are made into
drinking cups, and such as drink from them are attacked neither
by convulsions nor by the sacred disease [epilepsy]. Nay, they are
not even affected by poisons, if either before or after swallowing
them they drink from these cups wine, water, or anything else.*
– Ctesias, *Indica*, 5th century BCE

Ancient Greece and the Unicorn
The people of ancient Greece viewed the unicorn as a
marvelous creature, one that was a source of magical healing
through its glorious horn. This perspective is believed to have
been introduced by Ctesias, a Greek physician who served in
the court of Artaxerxes II of Persia. In the 5th century BCE,
Ctesias wrote about the mystical and magical attributes of
the unicorn in his book *Indica*, a compendium of beliefs that
the Persians had about India. One of the foremost details
about the unicorn that Ctesias presented to the Greeks was
the Asian idea of the unicorn's horn being a source of healing.
Ctesias' influential writings led to many Greeks adopting his
belief that the unicorn's magical horn had the ability to heal
numerous afflictions.

After Ctesias introduced the unicorn to the Greeks, some
intellectuals questioned whether there was sufficient proof
that the unicorn's horn had restorative properties. Aristotle,
an influential 4th century BCE Greek philosopher and
scientist, was one of those scholars who was suspicious of
Ctesias' claims, although Aristotle did believe that unicorns
existed. Unfortunately, Aristotle's skepticism about the
truly magical powers of the mythical unicorn's horn spread
amongst intellectuals in both Greece and Rome.

Rome and the Unicorn

Unlike Greece, ancient Rome was less open to free thought both generally and regarding the magical unicorn. Pliny the Elder was a 1st century CE Roman author, philosopher, natural historian, and military commander. Continuing from the body of scholarship established by Aristotle, Pliny the Elder furthered the minimization of the spiritual and healing aspects of the unicorn. Because of the misinformation that Pliny the Elder disseminated, fierceness started to become commonly attributed to the unicorn within both Roman and Greek sources.

Aelian, a Roman author from the 2nd and 3rd centuries, continued the Roman focus on stressing the description of the features of the unicorn and omitting its vital spiritual dimensions. Despite being erroneous in some of the details, Aelian, unlike Pliny the Elder or Aristotle, did understand that the unicorn's horn had restorative properties.

Further Perspectives

There were an assortment of unique perspectives about the unicorn that emerged from ancient Greek and Roman authors. Megasthenes, a Greek historian of the 4th and 3rd centuries BCE, learned of the existence of the unicorn from Buddhist monks and other contacts in the East. Because of confusion stemming from language and culture, Megasthenes believed that the unicorn was endowed with a combination of the features of a horse and a rhinoceros. Oppian, a 2nd century CE Greco-Roman poet, was the first known individual to state that unicorns were seen in Greece, claiming that unicorns inhabited the province of Aonia. Philostratus, a Greek teacher of the late 2nd and early 3rd centuries CE, asserted that when a person drinks from a cup made of unicorn horn for the remainder of that day they will become immune to illness, pain, poison, and can even walk through fire unharmed.

Face to Face with the Unicorn

Unlike most scholars of the Greco-Roman civilizations, who relied on outside information to draw their conclusions about the unicorn, some individuals from these cultures claimed to have seen the unicorn firsthand. Julius Caesar, the famed 1st century BCE leader of the Roman Republic, wrote in his book *Commentaries on the Gallic Wars* how he unexpectedly encountered a marvelous unicorn during a military endeavor in Germany's Hercynian Forest. Apollonius of Tyana, a 1st century Greek philosopher, had seen multiple unicorns while traveling in India. After returning to Greece, it is said that he was asked his thoughts on whether the unicorn's horn had the ability to resurrect the dead. In response, Apollonius of Tyana remarked that, "I should have believed it if I had found that the kings of this country [India] were immortal."

The Unicorn in Europe

In the heart of the forest a unicorn is born. The trees hold gentle branches around it, the forest pools guard its secret; only the stars can see. Among the silent spaces of the trees it grows protected, nurtured.

– Josephine Bradley, *In Pursuit of the Unicorn*

The Unicorn and the Celts

The Celts were a European people who are believed to have originated around 400 BCE. Greek historian Ephorus of Cyme speculated that their origins lay in the area around the Rhine River in Central Europe. The Celts would later spread to much of Europe, including Western Europe, the Iberian peninsula, and the United Kingdom and Ireland. The magical mythical unicorn had an important symbolic meaning to the Celtic people of Europe since before the common era. To the Celts, the unicorn represented the virtues of purity, endurance, fertility, gentleness, and it was associated with both nature and dreams. The Celts believed that the unicorn could look directly into a person's heart and know whether they were virtuous.

The Celts were an immensely spiritual people. They believed that the world of animals, the unicorn, and the world of humans were all interconnected. The Celtic alphabet is composed entirely of symbols which represent words. In this alphabet, the symbol for the unicorn also personified the solar year. The Celts had a unique astrological system. They included a zodiac sign for the unicorn, ascribed to individuals born between July 8th and August 4th. The unicorn sign represented balance of the Sun and Moon. Those born under this sign, which is today known as Cancer, were thought to be intelligent, loyal, and of service, and like the unicorn, natural caregivers with a generous spirit.

Like many other peoples, the ancient Celts believed that the unicorn's horn had the ability to counteract poison. They would place a unicorn horn on a table, and if the horn sweated, it indicated that the food was poisoned. The Celts believed the unicorn was a solar figure, and its horn was said to look like a flaming spear. To the Celts, the unicorn was a sacred creature that protected against evil and healed people.

The Wild People

5 – 15th century German playing card of a unicorn and wild woman.

The legend of the Wild People was a popular myth in many parts of medieval Europe. Known amongst themselves as the Old Ones, the Wild People were an oft-misunderstood group. Many Europeans were afraid of the Wild People because they were different, shunning them when they visited their towns and villages. The Wild People were said to live in forests, be covered in hair from head to toe, prefer nudity, sing and dance during thunderstorms and blizzards, avoid interactions with regular people, accompany the tinkermen in caravans, and have an extremely close relationship with the unicorn. The Wild People learned of the properties of healing herbs, the language of trees, and much secret lore from the magical unicorn. Travelers spun tales throughout Europe of the Wild People, especially Wild Women, riding the unicorn. Perhaps the close association of the Wild People with the unicorn was meant to show that the unicorn has always been drawn to those who were different.

The Fair Maiden and the Unicorn

Long ago, in the days before the throne of Scotland had been established, stood a decrepit castle in the remote Scottish Highlands. Inside the forlorn castle lived a beautiful maiden, nobility by birthright, who now had barely enough black bread to eat and clean water to drink. The maiden lived with her companions, a magical unicorn and an old crone who had been in her family's service and remained loyal after the passing of her parents. Their lives were difficult, but they worked together to ensure that their meager provisions were enough to provide their sustenance.

Though there were many challenges – not the least of which was the bitter cold of living in the castle, for its roof had long since deteriorated – the maiden did have an assortment of simple pleasures in her life. She and the unicorn enjoyed riding through the heather fields and up the rocky slopes of the large mountains of the Highlands. The maiden was partial to the feeling of the fresh mountain air blowing through her luxurious golden tresses and the unicorn was thrilled at the feeling of its hooves sliding over the snow-dusted peaks. When the ground became perilous from an overabundance of snow in the coldest months, the unicorn would dip its horn into the snow to melt it and ensure safe travel for the maiden and himself. One day, during one of their jaunts in the mountains, the maiden and the unicorn came across a band of hunters from a neighboring kingdom. The young men, having heard the legends of the magic of the unicorn and its horn, believed that if they could capture the horn, they could then cast a spell to attract the interest of the beautiful maiden. The young men lurked until the fair maiden dismounted and then aimed their deadly arrows at the unicorn, pulling back their bowstrings in unison. When the unicorn glanced in the hunters' direction and sensed their intentions, the young men instantly lost all feeling in their arms, their bows and arrows pitifully falling to the ground. While the maiden and the unicorn escaped back to the castle, the men sulked back to their land. Overcome with humiliation, they tried to convince themselves that the unicorn was only a horse and that its horn was a mere illusion. Furthermore, they consoled themselves with mistruths, spreading rumors of the fair maiden's hideous appearance to the local townsfolk.

When the maiden and the unicorn returned to the castle, shivering at the entrance were a band of Little People. Their leader, sensing the purity of the maiden and the unicorn, began to speak in a surprisingly loud tone of voice for one so diminutive in size. "Greetings, fair maiden and beloved unicorn of the dimensions where no mortal may traverse, unless they be of an opened eye. I am The Oldest and the Wisest, and my people are the Little People. We ask for your help. My people are tired and hungry and in dire need of shelter. The farm in which we inhabited was sold and the new owners demanded that we depart. I beseech you, fair maiden, may we reside in your home?"

The maiden was overcome with sorrow, hearing of the plight of the Little People. "I rejoice in helping you and your people, Much Honored Oldest and the Wisest, but I must ensure that the unicorn and the old crone who live with me shall also welcome your company."

The unicorn immediately spoke up, "I rejoice in helping you and your people."

"May we enter?" asked The Oldest and the Wisest.

"Certainly," replied the maiden, and the Little People, the unicorn, and the maiden entered the castle where they were greeted by the old crone. "You have been so loyal to me, my beloved unicorn, and my family, that I must ask if you would welcome the company of these poor travelers from a distant land."

The old crone nodded her head. "I rejoice in helping them."

And so, the Little People were escorted into the kitchen by the hearth, for most of the rooms of the castle were in grave disrepair and unsuitable for habitation. Weary from their journey, they rested, quickly drifting into sleep; the maiden, the unicorn, and the old crone retired to their rooms.

When the maiden woke up the next morning, she was astounded by the warmth of her surroundings. The winter gales did not whip against her body. When she looked up, she saw that the roof had been completely repaired. She gazed at the Little People in amazement, confused at what had transpired. The Oldest and the Wisest, seeking to allay her fears, said, "We welcome your generosity, and sought to repay you in kind."

"Thank you. Thank you so much," the maiden replied, to which The Oldest and the Wisest smiled as he tugged on his long gray beard.

The next morning, upon waking the maiden sleepily ambled into the kitchen for her usual slice of black bread. Rubbing her eyes, she noticed that the kitchen had been decorated in the manner befitting her noble birth. She raced through the entire castle and saw that her once decrepit home had been completely restored to its once proud bearing. The maiden shouted for joy, and out of a corner stepped the group of the Little People, their leader The Wisest and the Oldest speaking up, "We welcome your generosity, and sought to repay you in kind."

"How can I possibly repay you for the actions brought forth out of your warm hearts?" the maiden asked.

The Oldest and the Wisest replied, "Your happiness is sufficient, yet if you do wish to repay us, you may do so by accepting a word of advice."

"Certainly," replied the maiden.

"Your castle has been restored to its former glory. All that you now lack is a husband."

"A husband? Why, I have never even spoken to a man before." The maiden's face grew red with embarrassment as she realized that she had misspoken. Hoping not to offend her guests, she quickly added, "A man of the land, a human man. Though, of course, we are all one, but—"

The Oldest and the Wisest smiled, and his companions laughed. "I know your heart is pure, good maiden, so do not be concerned with the swiftness of language. I trust that a husband would provide love, partnership, and kindness."

"But how would I know which man is the right husband?" the maiden asked.

The Oldest and the Wisest chuckled. "Trust yourself, for I cannot provide all the answers for you, fair maiden."

"But there are few men in these lands. How could I even——?"

The Oldest and the Wisest remarked, "The birds of this land are our friends. I shall speak with the magpie, who can communicate with the osprey and the grouse, the red kite and the golden eagle, and they shall procure the best men of their lands." The Oldest and the Wisest then spoke to the birds, and the birds found the four best men of their lands, who all began to travel towards the maiden's castle.

The first to arrive was the Prince of the Frozen North. The maiden marveled at his courageous demeanor and handsome looks. She asked her suitor, "If you were to take my hand in marriage and rule this castle with me, would you allow the Little People to dwell with us?"

"The Little People," the Prince scoffed, "you naive girl, they no longer exist, and a good thing too, for they were known as the worst scroungers of the four winds."

The maiden frowned. "By the heartlessness in your response, you have proven that you are unsuitable to be my husband. Depart!"

The second to arrive was the Prince of the Warm South. The maiden marveled at his courageous demeanor and handsome looks. She asked her suitor, "If you were to take my hand in marriage and rule this castle with me, would you allow the Little People to dwell with us?"

"The Little People," the Prince scoffed, "you naive girl, they no longer live in our land, and a good thing too, for they were known as the worst beggars of the four winds."

The maiden frowned. "By the heartlessness in your response, you have proven that you are unsuitable to be my husband. Depart!"

The third to arrive was the Prince of the Eastern Seaboard. The maiden marveled at his courageous demeanor and handsome looks. She asked her suitor, "If you were to take my hand in marriage and rule this castle with me, would you allow the Little People to dwell with us?"

"The Little People," the Prince scoffed, "you naive girl, they drowned at sea years ago, and a good thing too, for they were known as the worst wanderers of the four winds."

The maiden frowned. "By the heartlessness in your response, you have proven that you are unsuitable to be my husband. Depart!"

The last to arrive was the Prince of the Western Isles. The maiden marveled at his courageous demeanor and handsome looks. She asked her suitor, "If you were to take my hand in marriage and rule this castle with me, would you allow the Little People to dwell with us?"

"The Little People," the Prince scoffed, "you naive girl, they never existed, and a good thing too, for they would be the worst vagrants of the four winds."

The maiden frowned. "By the heartlessness in your response, you have proven that you are unsuitable to be my husband. Depart!"

With the Prince of the Western Isles' departure, the maiden became distraught, for she imagined that all the birds of Scotland had failed in finding her a suitable partner. The next morning, the unicorn, the old crone, and the Little People gathered for breakfast, though the maiden was nowhere to be seen.

The old crone asked the unicorn, "Have you seen the maiden, Unicorn?"

"I have not," the unicorn replied. "Have you seen the maiden, The Oldest and the Wisest?"

"I have not," The Oldest and the Wisest replied. "But I do hear the sound of sobbing coming from her chamber. Let us ask what is the matter and then console her." And so The Oldest and the Wisest, all the Little People, the unicorn, and the old crone gathered together and headed to the maiden's chamber. "Fair maiden, what is the matter?" The Oldest and the Wisest asked in his booming voice.

The maiden answered the door. Through her tears and quivering voice, she explained, "None of the men were suitable, for all had cruelty in their hearts."

"Cruelty," The Oldest and the Wisest remarked. "Whatever do you mean, fair maiden?"

"All had contempt for you and your people, Much Honored Oldest and the Wisest."

The old crone placed her withered hand on the maiden's shoulder. "Be patient, dear. The right man shall come along soon enough."

"But where shall I find the right husband?" the maiden asked. At that moment, the old crone, The Oldest and the Wisest, and all the Little People turned to the unicorn. The maiden continued, "Oh, unicorn, if you were to take my hand in marriage and rule this castle with me, would you allow the Little People to dwell with us forevermore?"

"If I were your husband I would continue to treasure the Little People until the end of time and space," the unicorn replied.

"I do so wish you could be my husband," the fair maiden sighed. At that moment, the unicorn magically transformed into a man more handsome, more courageous, and far wiser than any of the maiden's four suitors. The maiden and the unicorn married, ruled the restored castle and lands justly, and lived happily and prosperously ever after with the old crone and the Little People by their side.

The Story of Isabel and Bartholomew

Perhaps no story better expressed the importance of the magical mythical unicorn in European chivalry than the tale of Isabel and Bartholomew. In medieval Europe, the unicorn served as a powerful emblem of chastity and kindness and was viewed as possessing the ability to defend itself honorably when necessary. These attributes led to the unicorn becoming emblematic of the code of chivalry associated with knighthood. Knights were expected to be true and serve, emulating the unicorn's inclinations.

Isabel was a princess celebrated for her beauty, grace, and abounding love for her prized unicorn. Her unicorn was a gift from her father, and she was known to exuberantly ride the unicorn throughout the hills, the forests, the shores, the towns, and every nook and cranny throughout her kingdom. Despite her father promising her in marriage to a prominent landowning knight, Isabel still attracted the attention of innumerable suitors drawn to her charms and position as the daughter of the king of Friesland in the Netherlands. Though the would-be suitors all possessed unique virtues, Isabel paid none of them any mind – except for Bartholomew. Bartholomew was a knight known for his unique abilities, including having been able to subdue a lion and turn the fierce animal into his companion. This impressive feat led to Bartholomew being nicknamed the Knight of the Lion. Whenever in Isabel's company, Bartholomew would shower her with affection, which Isabel accepted willingly. Isabel's betrothed privately seethed with anger every time she mentioned his rival. The knight knew that Isabel's heart belonged to Bartholomew and so he determined to create a ruse to separate them at any cost.

One day, Bartholomew went to visit Isabel at her castle. When Bartholomew arrived, a nervous page informed him that Isabel had died. Likewise, Isabel was told by a messenger dressed in Bartholomew's colors that Bartholomew had been killed in battle. Immediately upon hearing the messenger's pronouncement, Isabel fainted. The messenger fled from the castle with Isabel, having wrapped her inside a large rug to avoid detection. The fiendish messenger took Isabel to his master's imposing castle located on a remote cliff, where a dragon guarded the only entrance.

Several days later, while attempting to drown his sorrows with mug after mug of mead at his local tavern, Bartholomew overheard the knight's page tell his drinking companion that Isabel was not dead. After questioning the page about this rumor, Bartholomew learned that he had been ordered by the landowning knight on threat of death to inform Bartholomew that Isabel had died and that he had taken her to the knight's castle on the cliff. Bartholomew immediately decided to search for her. His affections for Isabel ran so deep that he was willing to accept any risk just to see her again. Like the great knights of lore, his duty and love knew no bounds.

After traveling to the distant castle, Bartholomew faced the dragon guarding the entrance. He soon realized that the dragon was a formidable foe. Even with his lion at his side, Bartholomew was no match for the flame-spewing dragon and stood in grave danger of losing his life. Sensing the peril that Bartholomew was facing, Isabel's magical unicorn appeared and came to his rescue. Upon seeing the unicorn, Bartholomew realized that this indeed was the place where Isabel was imprisoned. Given the danger of the situation, Bartholomew desired the help of Isabel's unicorn in confronting the fierce dragon. Understanding the rivalry between the unicorn and the lion, Bartholomew knew that if his lion and Isabel's unicorn could work in partnership, then the loathsome dragon could be defeated. The unicorn fought alongside Bartholomew and the lion, helping them to easily defeat the dragon. After they slayed the dragon, Isabel burst out of the castle, first embracing her magical unicorn, then Bartholomew. Having previously shoved the knight out of a high window with a well-timed push, Isabel showed Bartholomew the evil man's remains in the nearby moat. The pair were now united and returned to the castle. The King granted Bartholomew his daughter's hand in marriage and apologized profusely to Isabel for promising her to a wicked man. Forever after Isabel and Bartholomew were immortalized as the Lady of the Unicorn and the Knight of the Lion.

Katya and the Unicorn

The unicorn exerted a powerful influence throughout the whole of Europe. The story of Katya and the unicorn was a widely-told legend throughout Eastern Europe. The events that transpired in this story were said to have happened in the Crimean region of Russia.

In 1347, typhoid had struck a Crimean village. The villagers soon discovered that the source of the typhoid was the community well in the town center. Desperate for a solution, the villagers called a town meeting. At the meeting, one of the villagers shared with his fellow townsfolk the legend of how a unicorn's horn supposedly had the power to purify poisoned water and heal afflictions. After exhausting all other possibilities, the villagers fervently agreed to try to attract a unicorn, but were puzzled as to how to accomplish this feat. The only method that they had heard of was through an appeal to the unicorn's love of purity by luring it with a virgin. Unfortunately, at the first sign of the outbreak, the younger girls had left the village and the few older women that remained all had children. The villagers, misunderstanding the unicorn's love for purity of heart, assumed that the situation was bleak.

Katya, a mother of several children, was confident that she could attract a unicorn at the nearby steppe. Katya had visited the steppes near the village frequently as a child. One day, while singing a gentle song, she saw a magical unicorn out of the corner of her eye. When Katya told her parents, they did not believe her, yet Katya had no doubt in her mind that she had seen a unicorn. Remembering this event from her childhood, Katya hoped that the steppes would be the right place to start her search. She told the other women in the village of her plans, asking them to keep it a secret, and was met with much doubt. Though the women were skeptical of Katya's plan, they agreed to keep her secret, as the men of the village were known to be disreputable and not to be trusted with such a matter.

Once Katya reached the secluded area, she waited for the unicorn, singing the same beautiful song that she had sung in her childhood memory. The unicorn, hearing Katya's melodious song, approached her. Katya explained the village's plight, and recognizing the purity of her intentions, the unicorn agreed to travel with Katya back to the village. Upon their return, the unicorn dipped its horn into every bucket of water collected from the communal well and treated the sickest members of the village by placing its horn over their diseased bodies. The unicorn then eliminated the typhoid outbreak by purifying the waters of the well. Eternally grateful for its help, Katya led the unicorn back to the steppes, where they gleefully lingered for a number of days.

With the disease having been eradicated, the men of the village gathered together to discuss this miraculous event. Their village was not prosperous, yet its citizens had enough to meet their needs. Still, some of the men desired far more. Consumed with greed, a man named Sergius devised a scheme. He suggested that they kill the unicorn, sever its horn from its body, and sell the horn for an exorbitant profit. In case of a future outbreak in their village, they could keep a portion of the unicorn's horn as a safeguard. The men, filled with images in their mind of wealth and power, immediately consented to Sergius' plan. They gathered together the next morning and traveled to the steppes. When the men arrived, they saw Katya departing from her unicorn to head back home. "Attack," Sergius cried. At Sergius' command, one of the men distracted Katya, while the others rushed at the unicorn. The men killed the magnificent beast before it could defend itself against their ambush. In their greed, the men had sealed their fate.

This treacherous action against her cherished new friend shocked and horrified Katya. Unable to fathom the idea of living in a village with men whose hearts possessed such cruelty, Katya and her children immediately gathered their meager belongings and left the village and its evil men behind, never to return. The men continued with their plan, journeying to a nearby town known for its lucrative marketplace. In that prosperous town, they sold the horn for an immense profit of many sacks of gold. Like a band of wolves, the men immediately started to use their ill-gotten gains for savory foods, sweet fruits, potent drinks, fine clothes, and all manner of luxuries bought from the town's merchants. After returning to their village, the men gorged on their intoxicants before unloading the sacks of gold. Unbeknownst to them as they distributed their newfound wealth, plague-carrying rats had gnawed their way out of a crate of oranges and scurried into the village. Blinded by their insatiable lust for money, the men had forgotten to save a precautionary piece of the horn for their village. Within a few days, Sergius and the men all began to feel ill, with fevers, chills, and fatigue. Their wives, children, and the other villagers dismissed their complaints, assuming they had caught colds or a flu brought forth from the exertions of their travel, yet when the men all began to die, it was already too late. In a matter of weeks, every man, woman, and child in the village passed away from the plague. This tragedy could have been avoided; the village would have remained under the protection of the benevolent unicorn if only the men had chosen to reject Sergius' shortsighted and malicious plan.

The Unicorn Skeletons of Germany

During the 17ᵗʰ and 18ᵗʰ centuries there were three spectacular encounters with the skeletal remains of unicorns in Germany. In 1663, a group of workmen discovered the skeleton of a unicorn in a limestone quarry near the town of Quedlinberg. According to author Larry Brian Radka in his book *Historical Evidence for Unicorns*, the unicorn's horn at Quedlinberg was "as thick as a human shinbone and seven and a half feet in length." Author Anne Clark posits in her book *Beasts and Bawdy* that the skeletal remains of a unicorn and its horn were also found in the German town of Swedenburg in 1663. In the middle of the 18ᵗʰ century, the philosopher Leibniz recorded uncovering a unicorn skeleton in Germany's Harz Mountains. A former skeptic, after seeing the remains of a unicorn skeleton, Leibniz needed no further convincing of the proof of the unicorn's existence.

Modern European Traditions of the Unicorn

In the 20ᵗʰ century, the unicorn remained popular in contemporary Europe in various ways. Unicorn horns continued to be coveted due to their ability to heal. In 1905, mammoth bones were found in what was then Austria-Hungary's Slovak region. The workers who excavated this site were convinced that these were unicorn bones. The excavators kept many of these bones, wanting to believe that they were the bones of the unicorn because of the legendary claims of the unicorn's ability to heal.

The evil eye is a concept that appears throughout European cultures. It is thought that someone has been "given the evil eye" when someone speaks or wishes ill of them. Because of the unicorn's association with the Creator and with regenerative abilities, the unicorn's horn is thought to counteract the effects of the evil eye. In the town of Asturias in pre-World War II Spain, children were thought to be protected from the evil eye by the unicorn horn. Mothers and other caretakers in Spain would filter water with a horn fragment before they offered it to their children to drink. This practice was said to provide protection against the wicked thoughts and actions of others. In Greece, a similar tradition has been practiced in recent decades. There, children are guarded from the evil eye by a bone cross made of horn known as "monokero," which translates as unicorn. In Italy, the evil eye tradition takes a somewhat different turn. Outside of many Italian homes are heavy blocks of wood with a distinctive feature – a carved protruding horn. These wooden blocks, when placed against open doors, are assumed to keep demons away. Additionally, the necklace known as the Italian horn or cornicello, a protective amulet worn by many Italians, is also known as the unicorn horn. These traditions are but a few of the myriad ways that the unicorn continues to wield its magical power in Europe.

The Physiologus

The *Physiologus*, believed to have been written by an unknown author in Palestine around 370 CE, was one of the most widely read books in medieval Europe. The *Physiologus* taught Christian moral lessons through an assortment of fables that involved personified animals. Though the *Physiologus* adapted to local customs and trends in the many lands which it circulated, one constant in all traditions was the unicorn.

According to a 9th century Latin version of the *Physiologus* from Berne, the unicorn "is a small animal, like a kid, but exceedingly fierce, with one horn in the middle of his head; and no animal is able to capture him. Yet he may be taken in this manner: men lead a virgin maiden to the place where he most resorts and they leave her in the forest alone. As soon as the unicorn sees her, he springs into her lap and embraces her. Thus he is taken captive and exhibited in the palace of the King. In this way our Lord Jesus Christ, the spiritual unicorn, descended into the womb of the Virgin and through her took on human flesh." The New Testament of the Bible itself alludes to this connection between the unicorn and Christ, with the author of the gospel of Luke (1:69) writing of Zechariah's prophecy of the coming savior: "He hath raised up an horn of salvation for us in the house of his servant David." The unicorn's horn symbolizes spiritual oneness.

Much of the treatment of the unicorn in the *Physiologus* centered around what had become known as the water-conning story. In this story, a serpent would poison a body of water, which rendered it unfit to drink for the animals who depended on it for life. The beasts would wait for the unicorn to dip its horn in the poisoned waters, which magically purified them. After the unicorn had cleansed the water, the animals would once again be able to drink without harm. During a 1389 trip to Jerusalem, European travel writer Johannes de Hesse saw a unicorn dip its horn into a poisoned pool, purifying it. The *Physiologus* used this allegory as a metaphor for the power of Christ. One interpretation posited by Odell Shepard was that in the Christian version of this allegory the horn of the unicorn was seen to represent the cross, the serpent that poisoned the water denoted the Devil, and the poison symbolized the sins of the world, which were redeemed through Jesus Christ's martyrdom.

The *Physiologus'* influence extended far beyond Christendom. The unicorn story of the *Physiologus* had a major impact within the Islamic world. Unlike in the Christian versions of the *Physiologus*, the Islamic versions did not utilize the unicorn as a symbolic representation of Jesus. Muslims believe that religious figures cannot be depicted or symbolically portrayed, and so while the unicorn has long been celebrated by Muslims, its portrayal in the Islamic version of the *Physiologus* was without the religious significance ascribed to it in the Christian versions. Across cultures and faiths, the *Physiologus* spread the unicorn's mythology, and its impact was wide-reaching.

The Holy Hunt

Along with the water-conning story, one of the most popular fables involving the unicorn promulgated within the *Physiologus* was the Holy Hunt. In the *Physiologus'* version of the tale, a virgin would be utilized to lure a unicorn, since the unicorn was said to be receptive to purity and chastity.

The meaning of the Holy Hunt was subject to an assortment of interpretations. One common perspective was that the Holy Hunt presented how power could corrupt individuals to such a degree that they would kill the benevolent unicorn for personal gain. Royalty desired the unicorn's horn, as it was both a status symbol and had the invaluable ability to determine whether food and drink were poisoned. Additionally, many hunters longed for the mighty rewards that would be conveyed to them if able to kill the unicorn and retrieve its majestic horn.

The Holy Hunt was fostered by a misunderstanding of the symbolism of the unicorn and its horn. During the late medieval period, some Europeans started to view the Holy Hunt as a direct parallel for the story of the crucifixion and resurrection of Jesus Christ. To countless Christians of the time, the virgin represented Mary, the unicorn embodied Jesus Christ, and the unicorn's horn was symbolic of the unity of Jesus Christ and the Father. To adherents of this perspective, the unicorn was Christ consenting to be captured in order to die a physical death, resurrect, and thus cleanse humanity of its sins. This understanding of the Holy Hunt was widespread throughout Europe and had a unique expression in Germany.

Many German mystics celebrated the Virgin Mary as Maria Unicornis, or Mary of the Unicorn, and German churches were renowned for their frequent use of unicorn imagery.

The Unicorn in Africa

For the eastern side of Libya, where the wanderers dwell, is low and sandy, as far as the river Triton; but westward of that, the land of the husbandmen is very hilly and abounds with forests and wild beasts, for this is the tract in which the huge serpents are found, and the lions, the elephants, the bears, the aspicks, and the horned asses [unicorns].

– Herodotus, 5th century BCE

Prester John and the Unicorns of Ethiopia

There have been a multiplicity of Ethiopian myths about the unicorn. It has been said that magicians and alchemists of previous centuries were aware of the exceptional ability of the unicorn's horn to test for poison, believing that the horn would swell when brought into contact with harmful substances. The unicorn's horn was also utilized as a material to make bowls, goblets, and the handles of knives for Ethiopian princes. It was believed that unicorn horn-infused objects would protect Ethiopia's royalty from those who wished to do them harm.

According to legend, Prester John ruled the kingdom of Ethiopia from the 12th to the 17th centuries. Canadian-born esotericist Manly P. Hall stated that Prester John was a descendent of the Magi that foretold Jesus' birth. Prester John was known for his exceptional leadership and immense wealth. Unicorns were said to abound in Prester John's peaceful domain.

One of the most remarkable aspects regarding Prester John was that he was said to have possessed a herd of unicorns in his kingdom. Many of the historical reports of ownership of unicorns in the kingdoms of Africa, the Middle East, and India are thought to have been gifts from Prester John.

Despite the plentiful number of unicorns to which he was linked, Prester John considered the unicorns in his court only a mere fraction of the unicorns that inhabited his country. In Prester John's kingdom the unicorn was both respected for its might and freedom. No other animal was treated with as much reverence by Prester John and his people.

Accounts of the unicorns in Prester John's kingdom were confirmed by many witnesses, including Edward Webbe, an English traveler of the Elizabethan era, who remarked that he had seen 77 unicorns in the court of Prester John. John Bermudez visited Ethiopia in 1535 and reported that he had seen large unicorns that resembled horses at Prester John's court. Marmolius also saw unicorns at the court, describing them as akin to a young colt, though with a beard and large grooved horn.

Aside from within Prester John's court, there are multiple confirmed unicorn sightings in Ethiopia. Ludovico di Varthema was a 15th and 16th century author from Bologna in Italy who saw a unicorn in the city of Zeila, a place located in present-day Somalia, but which was then part of greater Ethiopia. Don Juan Gabriel, a Portuguese colonel, spotted a unicorn in the province of Damota in Ethiopia. Several Portuguese natives reported seeing unicorns feeding at the foot of the mountain in Ethiopia's Mountains of the Moon. Jieronymo Lobo, a Portuguese missionary of the 17th century, was also said to have seen unicorns while proselytizing in Ethiopia. These varied individuals confirmed a tradition of belief in the unicorn among Ethiopians.

The Unicorn in Egypt and North Africa
Egypt is a land known for its incredibly rich history within the mystical and wisdom traditions. Egyptian hieroglyphics have a symbol to represent the unicorn, showing that the unicorn has been an aspect of Egyptian civilization since

the culture's earliest days. Inside the pyramid at Memphis, there is a mural showing four antelopes and a unicorn being led by a man. This is only one of many mysterious esoteric depictions of the unicorn within the sacred structures of Egypt. This rich legacy of the unicorn in Egypt was made quite visible to Louys Paradis, a 16th century Parisian doctor, who stated that he saw a unicorn in Alexandria.

There are an assortment of myths about the unicorn in present-day Sudan and other regions in close proximity to Egypt. In Sudan, the unicorn is known as the u'nasa. The u'nasa is said to resemble a donkey in both shape and size, although it has a boar's tail and a single horn. The Tire Bina people of Sudan utilize the u'nasa and its horn as a cure and guard against poison.

South Africa

Many diverse groups of South Africans have expressed their beliefs in the unicorn. Both the Dutch-descended Boers and native Hottentots of South Africa have reported that they have seen unicorns and the Bushmen have similarly asserted the unicorn's existence. The belief in the unicorn amongst these South African peoples is part of a long tradition within the country; some of the nation's caves have ancient artwork that depicts unicorns.

The unicorn had long been a part of South African culture. In the mid-16th century, European explorer Garcias ab Horto had heard rumors that there were amphibian-like unicorns off the coast of South Africa and that the horns of these sea unicorns were a cure for illness. Three centuries after ab Horto, Sir Francis Galton visited South Africa. There, Galton learned from the Bushmen of the unicorn's presence in South Africa, as members of the group spontaneously mentioned the unicorn in conversation. The Bushmen remarked to Galton that the unicorn resembled a gemsbok in both shape and size, yet had a singular horn in the middle of its forehead that pointed forward. In a land renowned for its diversity, the unicorn has long been a magical part of the impressive tapestry that is South Africa.

The Unicorn in North America

Unicorn. Old French, unicorne. Latin, unicornis. Literally, one-horned: unus, one and cornu, a horn. A fabulous animal resembling a horse with one horn.
– Peter S. Beagle, *The Last Unicorn*

The unicorn has had a long presence within America. The early European explorers often interacted with the Native American peoples, who shared with them their legends about the magical unicorn. The Native Americans have long celebrated the virtues of the unicorn, often utilizing the unicorn's horn in spiritual and magical rituals.

News of the unicorn's existence in North America spread to Europe through the pens of various writers. Richard Hakluyt, an English writer of the late 16th and early 17th centuries, chronicled the explorations of the English explorers. In Hakluyt's accounts, he mentioned two encounters that European explorers had with the unicorn. Hakluyt mentions that Sir John Hawkins' record of his journeys to America included a passage where he engaged with Native Americans in Florida who wore pieces of unicorn horn in their necklaces. Hawkins wrote that, "Of these unicorns they have many; for that they doe affirm it to be a beast with one horne, which coming to the river to drinke, putteth the same into the water before he drinketh. Of this unicornes horne there are of our company, that having gotten the same of the Frenchmen, brought home thereof to show." Hawkins' account of the unicorn brings to mind the global legend of the water conning. Another European explorer of the Americas which Hakluyt mentioned had encountered the unicorn is John Davis. John Davis was known for exploring the east coast of North America. Davis noted the gifts he and his crew were given by the Native Americans, including "a darte with a bone in it, of a piece of Unicornes horne; as I did judge."

The voyages of the early European explorers led to news of the unicorn's presence in America filtering back to Europe. Arnoldus Montanus, a Dutch geographer, wrote *De Nieuwe en onbekende Weereld: of Beschryving van America en 't Zuidland*, an anthology of information about North, Central, and South America. Montanus' book was later translated into English and German, and spread the fact that the unicorn was one of the animals that inhabited the Dutch colony of New Netherland, which corresponded to the northeastern United States. Montanus wrote that, "On the borders of Canada animals are now and again seen, somewhat resembling a horse; they have cloven hoofs, shaggy manes, a horn right out of the forehead, a tail like that of a wild pig, black eyes, a stag's neck & love the gloomiest wildernesses; are shy of each other so that the male never feeds with the female except when they associate for the purposes of increase." Montanus' commentary on the unicorn was accompanied by an illustration of an assortment of animals, with the unicorn occupying the central position, as in many artistic works of the Garden of Eden.

In 1687, King James II of England, Scotland, and Ireland commissioned a seal for New York. On this seal, among other designs, were the shield with the British royal arms, upheld by the unicorn and the lion. The unicorn on New York's seal was adorned with a collar and chain, perhaps an allusion to one of the tapestries from *The Hunt of the Unicorn*. This seal represented New York for eighty years. Later American colonies would also adopt the unicorn in their seals, including Virginia and New England, a testament to the unicorn's wide-ranging presence in America.

The Unicorn in Heraldry

*The lion and the unicorn were fighting for the crown. The lion
chased the unicorn all 'round the town.*
– Popular British nursery rhyme

The Unicorn in British Heraldry

The mythical unicorn has long occupied an important place
in heraldic representations. Perhaps no land so emphatically
associates itself in heraldry with the unicorn as the United
Kingdom – particularly Scotland. The unicorn is thought to
have been introduced into Scottish heraldry by King Robert
III, who reigned from 1390 to 1406. King Robert III adopted
the unicorn onto the royal shield of Scotland after a series of
battles with the Norwegians and the English for independence.
According to author Skye Alexander in her book *Unicorns:
The Myths, Legends, & Lore*, King Robert III chose the unicorn
as a symbolic representation of Scotland because he believed
that the unicorn's valor, purity, and strength would inspire
his people. In 1480, King James III introduced the unicorn's
image onto gold coins used as currency that were known as
the unicorn and the half-unicorn.

**6 – Gold unicorn coin introduced by King James III of Scotland
in 1480.**

The unicorn was later adopted into Scotland's coat of arms and the Scottish national flag by Mary, Queen of Scots a few decades after King James III's death.

Many traditions place the unicorn in opposition to the lion. In Britain, this originally indicated the tension between Scotland, personified by the unicorn, and England, personified by the lion. In 1603, the Scottish and English thrones were

7 – The arms of King James I of Scotland and England (c. 1603–1625) symbolizing the union of the two crowns.

united under the reign of King James I of Scotland and England. To ease tensions and promote harmony between these newly aligned peoples, King James I of Scotland and England combined the unicorn and the lion in British heraldry in an allusion to the Biblical prophecy of peace in Isaiah 11:6.

Ever since then, these twin figures – the lion denoting might and the unicorn right – have jointly symbolized the United Kingdom in heraldry.

The Unicorn in Global Heraldry

The unicorn has been featured in numerous heraldic flags across the globe, including those of: the office of the President of Lithuania, the nation of Canada, the province of Nova Scotia in Canada, the province of Newfoundland and

8 – Seal of New England during the colonial period from Larry Brian Radka's *Historical Evidence for Unicorns*. The Latin reads: "Seal of New England in America. James II by God's grace king of Great Britain, France, and Ireland, defender of the faith."

Labrador in Canada, the province of Manitoba in Canada, the courts of British Columbia in Canada, the colonial-era seals of New England, New York, and Virginia in the United States, the city of Sorocaba in Brazil, the city of Eger in Hungary, the town of Saint-Lô in France, the town of Trushky in the Ukraine, the municipality of Menameradiel in the Friesland region of the Netherlands, the municipality of Ramosch in Switzerland, and the flags of several towns in Germany, Poland, Russia, and the Czech Republic. The unicorn was integrated into the heraldic coat of arms of many prominent individuals. King John I of Hungary, King David the Builder of the Republic of Georgia, the Italian Duke of Ferrara Borso d'Este, the Borromeo family of Italy, and the Baltic German Kruedener family are a few of the many individuals and families who incorporated the unicorn into their coat of arms. Many clerics, particularly in Austria, chose the unicorn as their personal emblem. They often owned large plots of land, and it was common for Austrian clerics to have their symbol represent the town that developed around their property. The unicorn was such a dominant part of European culture that many German publishers, printers, and bookmakers in the 16th and 17th centuries even utilized it as a trademark in their books. This fervor for the unicorn extended into 19th and early 20th century Africa, where many European companies that operated there integrated the unicorn into their heraldic brand. These companies were familiar with Africans' associations of the unicorn with prestige and valor, and the companies that used the unicorn in their logos dramatically outsold their competition.

The Unicorn in the Arts

Sometimes we all need a unicorn to believe in. Sometimes we need a unicorn to believe in us.
– Claudia Bakker

The Unicorn in Art

Since the dawn of civilization, the magical mythical unicorn has been well-represented in a magnificent variety of art. The unicorn has been depicted as a symbol in nearly all cultures, dating back to at least the cave drawings of the ancient South Africans and South Americans. According to Bruce Chatwin, author of *In Patagonia*, the nation of Argentina has an abundance of ancient artistic depictions of unicorns, including at Lago Posadas, Cerro del Indio, and the Cave of the Hands. An increasingly large number of these treasures of the ancient world continue to be rediscovered, allowing us a fuller picture of the importance of the unicorn across time.

9 – Bas-relief from the Sumerian civilization.

The Sumerians of ancient Mesopotamia are one of the first recorded civilizations. The city of Ur was one of the most important centers of Sumerian culture. Bas-reliefs that feature the unicorn have been recovered where Ur once stood. The unicorn was prominently included in Sumerian friezes that are believed to date to about the year 3100 BCE. These friezes display a group of Sumerians at leisure, with several unicorns nearby. The Sumerians also featured the unicorn on a stone seal, where the unicorn was engaged in agricultural work with several individuals.

Many of Egypt's greatest monuments included a symbol of the unicorn in their hieroglyphics, or cuneiform writing.

10 – Detail from an Egyptian papyrus of a unicorn and lion playing a board game.

Inside the pyramid at Memphis, there is a mural showing a man leading four antelopes and a unicorn. Inside a tomb at Beni-hasan, a unicorn was prominently displayed in an Egyptian wall-painting. According to Sir Edward M. Thompson, Principal Librarian of the British Museum, and Dr. EA Wallis Budge, Keeper of Egyptian and Assyrian Antiquities at the British Museum, this depiction at Beni-hasan shows a group of foreigners offering the unicorn as a tribute to Egyptian nobleman Khnemu-hetep.

The Assyrians of Mesopotamia were prolific in including the unicorn in their art. As a critically important symbol to the Assyrians, the unicorn was also placed in standards, flags that indicated the presence of kings or other political leaders. Assyrian cylinder seals displayed assortments of unicorns around the Tree of Life, an Edenic symbol held sacred in their culture. Esarhaddon, a king who reigned over the Assyrian Empire from 681–669 BCE, had the unicorn carved into a basalt stela alongside the Tree of Life. Ashurbanipal, the son of Esarhaddon, shared his father's reverence for the unicorn. Ashurbanipal commissioned a carved sculpture that depicted several unicorns. The kings of Assyria revered the sacred unicorn, honoring it by featuring the unicorn on their royal robes. The mythic unicorn's preeminence to Assyrian kings established an honoring of the unicorn amongst the wider culture. The unicorn was utilized on the painted bricks, walls, staircases, columns, and entrance of the palace at the Assyrian capital of Nimrud (also known as Calah). King Shalmaneser III, who reigned from 859–824 BCE, had a black obelisk erected outside his palace to honor the unprecedented territorial expansions of the Assyrian Empire under his reign; this impressive structure which is today exhibited in the British Museum included the unicorn. In the city of Carchemish on the Euphrates, two extraordinary monuments carved in stone featuring the unicorn have been recovered. One features the unicorn alone, whereas the other has the unicorn alongside animals and a male figure, much like the depiction in the Garden of Eden. A prominent motif in many Assyrian bas-reliefs was the hunt, where an Assyrian king hunted a unicorn with a bow and arrow, sometimes alone, and at other times alongside fellow hunters. This depiction most likely symbolizes a hunt for the spiritual essence of the unicorn. In later centuries, this motif would make its way into the art of Europe, where it was often misunderstood as a literal hunt.

The Babylonians held the mystical unicorn in extremely high regard and featured it in many of their artworks. Babylonian tablets and clay cylinders with cuneiform renderings of the unicorn have been recovered, signifying the importance of the unicorn within their culture. The unicorn was featured on a Babylonian seal alongside a multitude of animals that were being domesticated. In this seal the unicorn is alone, its head held high, not subject to the same treatment as the other animals. Spectacular art honoring Ishtar, the Babylonian goddess of love, beauty, and fertility, included the unicorn. The opulent Ishtar Gate, one of the entrances to the city of Babylon constructed by King Nebuchadnezzar II in approximately 575 BCE, prominently displayed hundreds of unicorns on its glazed brick reliefs.

The ancient Persians revered the extraordinary unicorn and included it in much of their finest art. Archaeologists have recovered many bas-reliefs that include the unicorn from the ruins of Persepolis. Sculptures of the unicorn being led by men in Persian attire have been recovered from Persepolis' ruins. According to author Larry Brian Radka in his book *Historical Evidence for Unicorns*, these sculptures are representations of

11 – The rock-cut façade of the tomb of King Darius of Persia (c. 522–486 BCE) from Larry Brian Radka's *Historical Evidence for Unicorns*.

the Persian Empire's dominance over the conquered lands of Media and Macedonian Greece. In Persia, the unicorn was honored by royalty. Over the Persian throne was a canopy that depicted numerous regal unicorns and lions. The palaces of King Darius the Great, who reigned from 522–486 BCE, and King Xerxes I, who reigned from 486–465 BCE, both featured the unicorn on impressive spiraled columns that supported the roof-beams of their palaces. King Darius the Great's tomb was adorned with magical unicorns, perhaps to assist him in transitioning into the next dimension. All of the staircases found in Persepolis' palaces and other structures depicted the unicorn, many of which paired it with the lion. The mystical unicorn was also included in the art on the exterior of a temple in the major Persian city of Susa, indicating a metaphysical use as an important symbol throughout the Persian Empire. The unicorn continued to be a popular source of inspiration for artists through the Islamic golden age of the 13th and 14th centuries, being depicted in Persian manuscripts, on glass vessels, and on miniatures. One 13th century Persian miniature displays the unicorn accompanied by three ring doves. There is a belief within Persia and throughout much of the Middle East that the unicorn is especially fond of the ring dove, and delights in its songs. Manuscripts retelling the adventures of Alexander the Great, known in Persia as Iskandar, have shown him riding triumphantly on his unicorn Bucephalus in battle against a variety of supernatural enemies.

In Greek art, the unicorn served as an important symbol of national protection, spirituality, and royalty. Currency in Mycenae artistically depicted the unicorn. Euphronios, a celebrated Greek artist believed to have been born around 535 BCE, portrayed the image of the unicorn on his elaborate vases and pottery. According to author Larry Brian Radka, the first king of Macedonia Caranus ordered that the unicorn be placed on the flag that represented the Macedonian Greek army. Radka's assertion is perhaps confirmed by the fact that a Macedonian bronze figure featuring the unicorn was excavated.

In South Asia, the civilizations of Mohenjo-daro and Harappa of the Indus Valley emerged in approximately 2600 BCE. Archaeologists have found seals of these cities that feature the unicorn. Scholar Premendra Priyadarshi stated that the sacred unicorn symbolized power and divinity to the peoples of the Indus Valley. A major aspect of most of the unicorn seals from these cultures was the presence of an incense burner, a ritual offering stand that was depicted underneath the head of the unicorn. In addition to frequently depicting unicorns on their seals, the Harappans added singular horns to other animals, including the tiger and elephant, using the single horn to indicate divine status and represent the awakening of the third eye.

The magical mythical unicorn has had a major presence within Vietnamese art. Since at least the beginning of the Nhà Lê Trung Hưng dynasty which reigned from 1533–1789, the unicorn (known in Vietnam as the ky-lan) has frequently been depicted in art within Vietnamese temples and on pagoda entrances. Small bronze ky-lans have been common adornments inside Vietnamese temples and pagodas. Owing to the ky-lan's status as an auspicious creature held in special esteem, these bronze ky-lans were often utilized as incense burners during religious rituals.

In the early 19th century under the Nguyen Dynasty, the ky-lan started to become more widely featured in art for Vietnamese royalty. Sculptures of the ky-lan were placed in palaces, as the ky-lan was believed to ensure loyalty and good behavior from those who attended to Vietnam's leaders. In 1886, Vietnamese rulers commissioned the creation of a golden seal to represent their kingdom; this seal featured the image of the ky-lan. Thirty years later, two more golden seals displaying the ky-lan were commissioned to further associate Vietnam with the ky-lan. Throughout the 19th and 20th centuries, the Emperor's footrest featured a ky-lan, signifying the close association of Vietnam's royalty with the magical mythical ky-lan. In the city of Hue, there are two stone ky-lans guarding the tomb of Emperor Minh Mang, who reigned from 1820–1840. Majestic bronze ky-lans can be found throughout Hue at numerous monuments, including at the Palace of Supreme Peace, the Ancestors Temple, the Longevity Palace, and the tomb of Emperor Thieu Tri, who reigned from 1841–1847. In Vietnamese art, the ky-lan has often been paired with other animals deemed auspicious. On top of the Palace of Supreme Peace, the ky-lan is paired with a dragon. On top of the Longevity Palace, the ky-lan is paired with a phoenix. To this day, the ky-lan continues to exert an influence on Vietnamese art, having been chosen as the symbol to represent Hue's annual cultural festival to the world.

The magical unicorn (known in China as the ki-lin) has been widely revered and frequently depicted in a variety of Chinese art forms. Chinese palaces and tombs have featured ki-lins made of bronze, stone, jade, and wood. Silk and paper paintings throughout Chinese history have regularly featured the ki-lin. Structural adornments made of wood, stone, and ceramics were utilized in Chinese architecture to decorate buildings. Wooden ki-lins were often displayed on screens and bell stands because of a longstanding belief in China that the ki-lin's beautiful voice resembles the harmonious pitch of a bell.

The unicorn has been a ubiquitous presence within European art. It has adorned paintings, tapestries, sculptures, king's thrones, heraldic symbols, stained glass windows, religious altars, sacred texts, books, choir stalls, pews, chests, doorways, jewel boxes, medals, and a wide variety of other items. These popular depictions have helped disseminate the unicorn myth throughout Europe.

The Unicorn Tapestries are a set of seven acclaimed

12 – "The Unicorn in Captivity," tapestry from *The Hunt of the Unicorn* tapestries at The Cloisters. This tapestry is believed to have been created circa 1500.

tapestries believed to have been commissioned in Holland around the year 1500. John D. Rockefeller Jr., an American business magnate and philanthropist, acquired these breathtaking pieces of art from the descendants of the noble French La Rochefoucauld family; and in 1937 Rockefeller donated *The Unicorn Tapestries* to The Cloisters, a museum in New York City that specializes in medieval European art. Upon receiving Rockefeller's donation, The Cloisters placed *The Unicorn Tapestries* on permanent exhibition because of their vital importance to European art. It has been said that after Rockefeller donated *The Unicorn Tapestries*, he regularly visited The Cloisters to gaze on the beauty of the magical unicorn.

The following myth is an allegory depicting the essence of the story of the seven tapestries of the European holy hunt presented in *The Unicorn Tapestries*. Cassandra was a beautiful young woman, renowned for her honesty, purity, and kindness. Although she was esteemed by all the townsfolk, whispers about Cassandra's seemingly odd behavior had started once she began to regularly linger in the nearby forest. Her brother Evert, a prominent nobleman, was embarrassed by the rumors about the strange behavior of his sister, and confronted Cassandra about her mysterious lingering in the forest. "What could the forest offer that would be so profound that you should tarry every day amongst the wild beasts?" Cassandra did not wish to reveal her secret to her impetuous brother, yet could not overcome her truthful nature. "Why, brother, I saw the wondrous unicorn amidst the serenity of the trees, its magnificent spiraled horn deep in the stream, and the creatures of the forest assembled there to drink."

Evert knew his sister to be honest in all her words and deeds. While the thought of a magical unicorn having appeared to his sister seemed far-fetched, Evert did believe that his sister thought she had seen the elusive unicorn.

Secretly following her the next day, Evert observed that his sister had indeed seen the unicorn, seeing it for himself from his hidden place behind the trees. Remembering that the King desired a unicorn's horn, a dastardly thought ran through Evert's mind. *If my men capture this elusive beast, I shall impress the King when I present it as a gift, and thereby advance my standing by offering the horn which he seeks.* The next day Evert assembled a band of his knights and finest hunting dogs, and he and his party ventured into the forest. When they reached the stream that wound through the forest, Evert and his men followed its path until they came upon a majestic fountain that had been built to honor the memory of their father, who had served as the previous king and was a man known for his generosity of spirit. There was the magical unicorn, its horn in a gentle stream, with a variety of animals drinking from the placid waters. The beauty and serene gaze of the majestic unicorn temporarily stunned Evert and his men.

Evert cried out, "Attack!" The men and their greyhounds advanced towards the unicorn, their spears in hand. Faced with this threat, the unicorn sought to flee. The size of the group assembled left the unicorn trapped. While the unicorn is a peaceful creature, it did defend itself against this frenzied attack. The unicorn plunged its horn into one of the men's dogs, a wound that disabled the animal, yet did not kill it. It then cleared a path for itself through some of Evert's men. For Evert, as he watched the courageous unicorn escape, he saw the entirety of his future dissipating before his eyes.

Evert was an ambitious man, one not content to remain in his current position forever, elevated as it was. Desperate for his advancement in the King's court, Evert developed an idea to attract the unicorn once more. Aware that his sister had already made the acquaintance of the unicorn, Evert knew that if he could once again follow Cassandra into the forest without her knowledge, then he and his men could unexpectedly spring upon the unicorn. The next day, while Cassandra sat to a breakfast meal of porridge and bread, Evert approached her. "My sister, I must ask, do you plan to visit that beloved forest today?"

Cassandra replied, "I do, good brother, for I so love the magical unicorn of the enchanted forest."

"I long to have such an encounter. We must visit the forest together and see this glorious creature. May I accompany you?"

"As you wish, good brother, for I do so long to see my companion."

"I am pleased, dear sister. We shall head out after midday." Having convinced Cassandra to let him accompany her, Evert alerted his men of what was to transpire.

Cassandra led Evert through the forest to the stream, rejoicing in her brother's interest in observing the magical unicorn. Following behind, too distant to be noticed by Cassandra, were Evert's men. "Where does the unicorn dwell, dear sister?"

"There is a special place where I engage the unicorn, good brother. We meet in our family's garden by the banks of the stream. We shall travel there, and I trust that we will encounter my beloved unicorn."

As they continued to head towards the unicorn and Cassandra's special place, Evert intentionally tripped over a rock, skinning his knee. "Dear sister, I am afraid that I must see this marvelous beast another time, but please continue, for I would not dare to dream of disrupting your enjoyment of this wondrous creature."

"Can I be of service, good brother?"

"It is but a wound, dear sister. I shall not disturb what brings you such joy."

Cassandra smiled, kissing her brother on the cheek, and went on her way. Evert signaled his men, who crept out from behind the trees where they were lurking and continued in their march through the forest. Evert propped himself off the ground, wiping the blood off his knee, and addressed them. "Cassandra says that the unicorn shall be in the garden by the stream. We shall slay the unicorn there. I will receive the appropriate patronage of the King and your allegiance shall be remembered as my esteem grows."

When the men arrived at the garden, Cassandra was gently talking to the magical unicorn, so transfixed by its purity and kindness that she did not notice the forward creeping of the men towards her beloved friend. Encircling the garden, the men came upon them and pierced the unicorn's flesh with their spears, instantly taking the life out of the body of the magical unicorn. Cassandra wept, and Evert sought to console her. "Dear sister, I am aware of your love for the unicorn, yet rejoice in the fact that we shall have new luxuries and be held in the highest esteem by our King. Surely, that is worth more than mere friendship with that beast."

"You do not understand, good brother. I shall choose to remain in this forest all of my days, for the unicorn's spirit abides here, and I have never felt such compassion, such love, such kindness, such purity, as that of the unicorn."

"As you wish, dear sister." Evert turned to the men. "We must take the horn back to the castle and receive our rewards."

When Evert presented the unicorn's horn to the King, it was cause for a lively celebration. There was much dancing and revelry, and a great feast which was partaken in by all, from the King to the lowest of the townsfolk. Evert basked in the adoration of the crowd yet evaded the question when asked why his sister did not choose to attend the gathering. In time, seeing that his sister upheld her word to never return to the castle, Evert began to realize the abhorrent nature of his action and died of grief shortly thereafter. Cassandra, remaining in the garden, lived far longer than her brother.

While Cassandra never returned to the castle, she spent the remaining thirty-three years of her life deep in the forest, where no men dwelled, enjoying the spiritual essence of the unicorn.

The Lady and the Unicorn, currently on display at Paris' Musée de Cluny – Musée national du Moyen Âge, are a set of six tapestries that feature a noblewoman with a unicorn on her left side and a lion on her right side. The unicorn represents her internal self, while the lion represents her external presentation. These tapestries are thought to have been commissioned by Jean Le Viste, an influential nobleman in the court of King Charles VII of France.

The most striking feature of these tapestries is the esoteric symbology represented in the interactions between the Lady and the unicorn. The first tapestry in the set has the Lady clasping the unicorn's horn with her left hand, while holding a pennant with her right hand. The unicorn's horn in the Lady's left hand is symbolic of the opening of the third eye, suggesting the process of conscious awakening. The Lady's pennant in her right hand is adorned with three crescent moons, connecting it to the lunar energies that symbolize the feminine principle expressed in the goddess tradition. Metaphysical principles indicate that one is to draw into with the left side and make manifest externally through the right side, which directly connects with the artist's positioning of the horn in the Lady's left hand and the banner in her right hand. The next three tapestries in this set feature the unicorn and the lion each holding one of the Lady's banners. The unicorn and the lion have historically represented polarized properties (e.g. moon and sun; feminine and masculine; conscious and unconscious; etc.). The artist is encoding through the symbolism in these tapestries the need to unify opposite traits, as in the alchemical process, in order to transform and ascend. In the fifth tapestry, the Lady caresses

13 – "Touch," the first tapestry in *The Lady and the Unicorn* exhibited at Paris, Musée de Cluny – Musée national du Moyen Age. These tapestries are believed to have been created in the late 15th century.

the unicorn with her left hand while holding a small mirror with her right hand. The mirror does not show an exact reflection of the unicorn, but rather the purity and beauty of its essence, which she is now able to see through her opened third eye. The final tapestry in the set has the phrase "*À Mon Seul Désir*," which translates to "Love desires only beauty of soul," written on the Lady's noble canopy which represents her now higher consciousness. In this tapestry, the Lady puts a necklace into a chest held by her maid, symbolizing a shift in her understanding of the external trappings of beauty and

14 – "Taste," the second tapestry in *The Lady and the Unicorn* exhibited at Paris, Musée de Cluny – Musée national du Moyen Age.

15 – "Smell," the third tapestry in *The Lady and the Unicorn* exhibited at Paris, Musée de Cluny – Musée national du Moyen Age.

16 – "Hearing," the fourth tapestry in *The Lady and the Unicorn* exhibited at Paris, Musée de Cluny – Musée national du Moyen Age.

17 – "Sight," the fifth tapestry in *The Lady and the Unicorn* exhibited at Paris, Musée de Cluny – Musée national du Moyen Age.

18 – "Á Mon Seul Desír," the sixth tapestry in *The Lady and the Unicorn* exhibited at Paris, Musée de Cluny – Musée national du Moyen Age.

love and a commitment to a deeper truth, that love desires only beauty of soul. These six tapestries are an artistic rendition of a coded message showing the Lady progressively ascending towards enlightenment, having unified her external and internal. Like the Lady of these artworks, those able to decipher the tapestries were reminded that enlightenment comes from a unification of opposites. Although difficult to do in a culture where the feminine and lunar spiritual energies are suppressed, when this spiritual journey is pursued higher consciousness awakens and balance is attained.

Artistic works that feature the unicorn often present spiritual connotations through symbolism. In European art, the unicorn has traditionally served as a symbol for purity, virtue, love, and transformation. One such representation

19 – Antonio Pisanello's "Lady with Unicorn" medal commissioned by Cecilia Gonzaga circa 1447.

to that effect was Renaissance-era Italian artist Giorgione's *An Allegory of Chastity*, in which a unicorn rests its head in the lap of a maiden. The Gonzaga medal, 15th century Italian artist Pisanello's commissioned work for noblewoman Cecilia Gonzaga, features a unicorn resting at a woman's feet. Italian artist Raphael portrayed a woman and unicorn together in his *Portrait of Young Woman with Unicorn*. Raphael's unicorn is docile as a graceful woman cradles the youthful unicorn in her arms. In these works of art, Giorgione, Pisanello, and Raphael were indicating the bond that has long existed between the magical unicorn and the pure of heart maiden.

European artists of the Renaissance era frequently depicted the Edenic paradise in their artworks. Raphael's painting *The Creation of the Animals* and German artist Lucas Cranach the Elder's painting *Paradise* both featured the Great Creator presiding over a diverse assortment of animals in Eden, including the magical mythical unicorn. An acclaimed Flemish tapestry shows Adam and Eve naming the animals in the Garden of Eden. The animals displayed in this tapestry are in pairs, except for the singular unicorn, an indication of its preeminence. These artworks remind us that the magical unicorn has been present with humankind since the beginning in the higher dimensions, before humanity's fall to a lower vibration.

In Europe, the widely revered unicorn was depicted within many sacred structures. The Romanesque and Gothic stained glass windows of European cathedrals and churches often featured unicorns amidst traditional allegorical scenes. Carvings and paintings of the unicorn were common in medieval European places of worship, including in France's Strasbourg Cathedral, Germany's Grimmenthal Church, and a multitude of other cathedrals and churches throughout Europe. During the 15th century, some European places of worship began to feature the unicorn on their altars. In Germany, one such altar depicted the Holy Hunt, and was believed to have had the power to heal the sick. Author Nancy Hathaway states that this altar attracted tens of thousands of pilgrims annually, many of whom reported miraculous healings.

Historical psalters (collections of the Book of Psalms from the Judeo-Christian Bible) and devotional books of hours (collections of psalms, prayers, and other texts) from Europe often included illustrations of the transcendent unicorn. One of history's most notable books of hours was the one created for King James IV of Scotland, who reigned from 1488–1513. An illustration within this book of hours shows the King bowing before the two unicorns of the royal Scottish arms.

Art in a variety of medieval European books regularly featured the mythic unicorn. One example is the illustrations in *Travel to the Holy Land*, a book written by Bernhard von Breydenbach, deacon of Germany's Mainz Cathedral. *Travel to the Holy Land* featured reproductions of woodcuts of the unicorn created by Dutch artist Erhard Reuwich. Reuwich's

**20 – King James IV of Scotland kneeling before two unicorns
from a Flemish book of hours made for James IV, circa 1505.**

art accompanied the description of a unicorn sighting near
Mount Sinai. Edward Topsell, a 17th century English cleric
and author, published an encyclopedia of animals titled
Historie of Foure-footed Beastes. Topsell was an adamant
defender of the mythical unicorn's existence, stating within
his book that, "God himself must needs be traduced, if there
is no unicorn." Topsell's description of the creature included
eleven illustrated pages of the unicorn.

A unique artistic depiction of the unicorn was created by
the 20th century surrealist artist Salvador Dalí. Dalí's bronze
sculpture of a unicorn, its horn piercing a hole in a brick wall
to make wine, is exhibited on the grounds of the Château

de Pommard winery in Burgundy, France. The unicorn's presence in European art has traditionally been extremely diverse.

The unicorn, or karkadann as it is known in the Middle East, has been a popular figure within the art of the Islamic-era Middle East. Many noteworthy bestiaries, including those of al-Kawzini, ibn Bukhtishu', Ibn al-Durayhim al-Mawsili, al-Djahiz, and Ibn Ghanim al-Maqdisi, all featured elaborate illustrations accompanying their descriptions of the karkadann.

Throughout the Islamic world, the unicorn has had a presence in the arts. During the Muslim-ruled Mughal period of India in the 17th century, fabulous carpets were woven with the unicorn at their center. These carpets often adorned royal palaces and fine mosques. In Persia, various manuscripts were illustrated with the unicorn. One such manuscript, believed to be from the 16th century and presented by HR d'Allemagne in his book *Du Khorassan au Pays des Backhtiaris*, has an assortment of animals approaching mullah Djami, a Sufi religious leader, to report the ill treatment they have received at the hands of humanity. The unicorn and elephant defend and lead these animals in their pursuit of justice.

At the National Museum in Damascus, Syria is a stunning enameled terracotta unicorn bowl that is believed to trace back to the 13th or 14th century. In the bowl's center is a unicorn with a magnificent horn lying in green grass. On the unicorn's right side is a sun and some experts believe a moon is shown on the unicorn's left side. While the unicorn in this bowl is traditionally depicted, many medieval Islamic art objects show the unicorn with wings. These winged depictions include a 13th century bronze canteen and a 14th century glass vessel from Syria. Perhaps the Buraq, or winged equine from the Qur'an that transported the Prophet Muhammad with the angel Gabriel to the farthest mosque (often believed to be in the seventh heaven), could potentially be a variation of the unicorn. Across time, culture, and spiritual tradition, the unicorn's presence has always been important within global art.

The Unicorn in Plays

The written word is one of the greatest tools that humankind has utilized for illumination, information, instruction, and entertainment. The magical mythical unicorn has inspired countless works of literature, including plays, poems, novels, and all types of writing. William Shakespeare, arguably the most well-known and acclaimed writer of any era, frequently utilized the unicorn symbolically. As a playwright, Shakespeare alluded to the unicorn in *The Tempest*, *Julius Caesar*, and *Timon of Athens*. In *The Tempest*, the normally sardonic Sebastian exclaims, "Now I will believe that there are unicorns," signifying that he has cast his doubt aside after being witness to a supernatural occurrence. Knowing that the real-life Julius Caesar encountered a unicorn in Germany's forests and that he later retold this experience, Shakespeare interjected the following line in his play *Julius Caesar*. Decius remarks, "I can o'ersway him. For he loves to hear that unicorns may be betrayed with trees... and men with flatterers," part of a passage that indicates that Decius believes that Caesar is gullible. In *Timon of Athens*, the heroic Timon informs Apemantus that "wert thou the unicorn, pride and wrath would confound thee and make thine own self the conquest of thy fury," meaning that even if Apemantus inherently possessed a purity equal to that of the unicorn, he would still find a way to be trapped in superficial illusion.

American playwright Tennessee Williams chose to feature the unicorn in his play *The Glass Menagerie*, which first premiered in 1944. Laura, one of the main characters of Williams' play, is a demure woman with low self-esteem.

Laura's only comfort is her collection of glass figurines, particularly her unicorn. Laura sees a companion in the unicorn figurine, for it too is different from its peers by virtue of its singular spiraled horn and the spiritual properties which the unicorn and its horn represent. In this play, Laura's glass unicorn loses its horn after the figurine accidentally falls off her shelf. This destruction of the majestic unicorn figurine is thought to serve as a metaphor for Laura's feelings of loss of power and hopelessness.

Late 19th and early 20th century Irish poet and dramatist William Butler Yeats illustrates the transformational energies of the unicorn in his play *The Unicorn from the Stars*. Yeats' unicorns, responding to the political and social stagnation of the world, serve as destructive forces against that stagnation in order to rebuild the world anew. Yeats symbolically expressed that without the cathartic efforts of the unicorns, the world (as presented in his play) would remain forever in destructive stagnation.

The Unicorn in Poetry

It is said that poetry is the language of the soul, a beautiful art form rife with symbolism; therefore it is understandable that the magical mythical unicorn has often been a source of inspiration for many poets.

"The Unicorn" is a poem by Rainer Maria Rilke, a Bohemian-Austrian poet. Rilke's poem details an encounter between a unicorn and a holy man. The unicorn unexpectedly appears before the holy man, who is occupied in prayer. Aware of what the unicorn represents, the holy man immediately becomes reverent towards both the marvelous unicorn and its majestic horn.

Palestinian poet Tawfiq Sayigh's poem "A Few Questions I Pose to the Unicorn" has been described by critic and modernist poet Jabra Ibrahim Jabra as, "the strangest and most remarkable poem in the Arabic language." Sayigh's poem details the rich history of the unicorn. One excerpt translated by Zahra A. Hussein Ali in her article "The Aesthetics of Dissonance: Echoes of Nietzsche and Yeats in Tawfiq Sayigh's Poetry" from the *Journal of Arabic Literature* reads:

In our inaugural dawn,
In the pageantry of conferring names
When the legions streamed
Past the dais,
All animals, like parades, paired together.
You headed the pageantry
Without a mate.
All felt whole, contented.
Marching in uniform stride.
You led them alone
Like the horn in the middle of your head;
Trippingly, with anxious steps.
You searched with sight and sniff
For her, the never-to-be-found even
In Highest Paradise.
In the magnificent dawn,
In the sweeping pageantry,
Only you and God were solitary.

WH Auden, an English-American poet, petitions with the unicorn to awaken humankind in his poem "New Year Letter." In this poem, Auden writes of humanity's tendencies towards negligence and pride, with the hope that the unicorn will open people's hearts and transform their lives.

Anne Morrow Lindbergh, American poet, aviator, and wife of aviator Charles Lindbergh, beautifully elaborates on the essence of the final panel of *The Hunt of the Unicorn* tapestries in her poem "The Unicorn in Captivity." Lindbergh's poem was part of an anthology of poetry written from 1935 to 1955, after the kidnapping and death of her son.

Puerto Rican-American poet William Carlos Williams presented the marvelous unicorn as beyond comparison in an excerpt from his voluminous epic poem "Paterson," writing that:

The Unicorn
has no match
or mate.

Theobald I of Navarre, a 13th century Spanish king renowned for his verses, referenced the unicorn's pull towards the pure maiden in his poem "Licorne de Thibaut de Champagne," writing that:

The unicorn and I are one:
He also pauses in amaze
Before some maiden's magic gaze,
And while he wonders, is undone.
On some dear breast he slumbers deep
And Treason slays him in that sleep.
Just so have ended my Life's days;
So Love and my Lady lay me low.
My heart will not survive this blow.

Traditional Middle Eastern poetry, known as qasidah, often featured the karkadann (unicorn). One myth about the karkadann shown in the qasidahs was the global water-conning story, which expresses how the horn, which represents spiritual oneness, can cleanse impurities. This is an allegory for how the opened third eye cleanses and purifies. Pre-Islamic Arabian poet Alqamah ibn Abadah wrote of the water-conning legend in one of his poems.

These are only some examples of the many poets whose fondness for the unicorn inspired them to weave this magical creature into their poetry. William Shakespeare, CS Lewis, Labid, Edmund Spenser, Audre Lorde, Dylan Thomas, and Federico García Lorca are a few of the many other poets who have also been drawn to the mystical unicorn.

The Unicorn in Novels and Short Stories

A wide assortment of novels and short stories have featured depictions of the magical mythical unicorn. Peter S. Beagle's *The Last Unicorn* is one of the most well-known portrayals of the unicorn in literature. The main character in this novel is a female unicorn named Unicorn who believes that she is the last one of her kind. Once Unicorn learns that an evil animal named Red Bull captured the other unicorns and led them away from their natural dwelling, she knows that she must journey on a quest to find and rescue the other unicorns. Even though Unicorn was successful in her undertaking in *The Last Unicorn*, Beagle wrote a sequel entitled *Two Hearts* which continues the saga and reveals the fate of Unicorn and her companions. Beagle was prolific in his writings about the unicorn, penning three other works, including: *The Unicorn Sonata*, *Julie's Unicorn*, and *The Last Unicorn: The Lost Version*.

La Guerra Del Unicornio [The War of the Unicorn], a novel written by Mexican author Angelina Muñiz-Huberman, is an allegorical retelling of the Arthurian legends set in a fantastical version of medieval Spain. In Muñiz's novel, a conflict rages between the Knights of Gules, who are committed to building a just kingdom, and the Knights of Sable, who seek to create a tyrannical empire. In place of the Holy Grail of Arthurian folklore, the Knights of Gules embark on a quest to find the unicorn, which is used in the novel to symbolize the Holy Spirit. Don Álvaro, a knight who leads the Knights of Gules, seeks out the assistance of two holy men who have encountered the unicorn: Yucuf, a Muslim alchemist who has successfully transmuted base metal into gold by utilizing powder from the unicorn horn, and Abraham, a Jewish mystic who has united with the divine. The unicorn appears multiple times before Don Álvaro, portending his destiny as leader of this diverse land. Don Álvaro ultimately steps into his destiny when Yucuf gives him the unicorn's horn. After receiving the horn, Don Álvaro receives mystical powers which enhance his prowess in the battlefield. Despite the unicorn revealing itself to Don Álvaro, the Knights of Gules are ultimately unsuccessful in their battle against the Knights of Sable. Muñiz ends her novel with the unicorn retiring to the top of a mountain with Mara, Don Álvaro's love interest and the unicorn's favorite companion. In a bittersweet ending, the people, though suffering in the present, are hopeful that one day the unicorn will make itself known again by anointing a new hero who will succeed in creating a just kingdom.

Stardust, a graphic novel written by British author Neil Gaiman with illustrations by American artist Charles Vess, draws on a multitude of legends about the unicorn. Tristran Thorn, *Stardust*'s protagonist, saves a mystical unicorn from a fierce lion. After being rescued, the unicorn places its head in the lap of Yvaine, a maiden from the stars, and becomes her companion. Later in the novel, the unicorn protects Tristran by removing poison from a glass of wine with its horn, and shields Yvaine and Tristran from the malicious intentions of an evil witch. In the original graphic novel, the unicorn is defeated by the witch, who removes its horn and keeps it for its healing value; however, in the film adaptation the unicorn defeats the witch.

British novelist JK Rowling integrates the unicorn in various ways into her *Harry Potter* novels. In these books, drinking unicorn's blood grants immortality; however, there is a major caveat – any individual who slays a unicorn to acquire its life-giving blood becomes cursed. Firenze, an ally of hero Harry Potter, explains: "You have slain something pure and defenseless to save yourself, and you will have but a half-life, a cursed life, from the moment the blood touches your lips." Lord Voldemort, the principal antagonist in *Harry Potter and the Sorcerer's Stone*, utilizes unicorn blood to strengthen himself while on the verge of death and suffers the consequences for his selfish action. While unicorn blood offers immortality, unicorn hair has a different purpose in the *Harry Potter* series, being utilized to construct extremely powerful magical wands. Since the unicorn is a loyal and mystical creature, its wands are similarly known for faithfulness to their owners, skill in casting spells that benefit the greater whole, and defending against black magick.

Roger Zelazny, an American author, features the magical unicorn in his *Amber* series of novels. In the *Amber* series, Zelazny has the unicorn serve as a symbolic embodiment of the universal concept of cosmic order. Zelazny utilizes the serpent to represent chaos in his works. This contrast between the unicorn and the serpent harkens to the legend associated with the Garden of Eden, where the unicorn was blessed by the Creator, given the power of consciousness, and became the first animal named, whereas the serpent led humankind into the fall through deception.

British children's novelist Geraldine McCaughrean's book *Unicorns! Unicorns!* draws inspiration from Jewish folklore about the unicorn. In *Unicorns! Unicorns!*, McCaughrean's unicorns save animals from the worldwide flood by helping them get to safety on Noah's ark.

In novels and short stories, one of the most frequent ways the unicorn is depicted is through the symbology of the lion, representing the body, and the unicorn, representing the soul. *The Brave Little Tailor* by German authors the Brothers Grimm is a symbolic retelling of the myth of the battle between the unicorn and the lion. This symbolism also influenced English author Lewis Carroll. In Carroll's *Through the Looking-Glass*, a unicorn and a lion are fighting for the crown, perhaps a reference to King James I's unification of England symbolized by the lion, and Scotland symbolized by the unicorn. An alternative theory about what Carroll was representing through the unicorn and the lion was put forth by author Skye Alexander in her book *Unicorns: The Myths, Legends, & Lore*. Alexander suggests that Carroll was referring to the political skirmishes between William Gladstone, leader of the Liberals, and Benjamin Disraeli, leader of the Conservative Party within the British parliament. Alexander provides further evidence for this point in the consistent referrals of the unicorn and the lion in other British political writings, including Richard Aldous' *The Lion and the Unicorn: Gladstone vs Disraeli*, George Orwell's *The Lion and the Unicorn: Socialism and the English Genius*, and Sir Arthur Bryant's *The Lion and the Unicorn: A Personal History of Twentieth-Century England*.

British novelist CS Lewis included a magical unicorn named Jewel in *The Last Battle*, the final installment of his *Chronicles of Narnia* series. In this book, for her efforts on behalf of good, Jewel is allowed to enter the paradise of the god figure in the series, the Great Lion Aslan.

The following is a list of some of the many additional novels and short stories that feature the unicorn: Piers Anthony's *Apprentice Adept* novels, Robert Asprin's *Myth* novels, Terry Brooks' *Landover* series, Bruce Coville's *Unicorn Chronicles*, Janice Elliott's *The Birthday Unicorn*, Elizabeth Goudge's *The Little White Horse*, Jay Halpern's *The Jade Unicorn*, Edward D. Hoch's *The Last Unicorns*, Dorothy P. Lathrop's *The Colt from Moon Mountain*, Madeline L'Engle's *A Swiftly Tilting Planet*, Iris Murdoch's *The Unicorn*, Andre Norton's *Year of the Unicorn*, Fletcher Pratt's *The Well of the Unicorn*, Francois Rabelais' *Pantagruel*, Martin Walser's *Das Einhorn*, TH White's

The Once and Future King, Phyllis Whitney's *The Golden Unicorn,* and many others. Future generations of writers will surely continue to draw inspiration from the magical mythical unicorn and the wealth of imagery and symbolism associated with this glorious creature.

The Unicorn in Film

The beauty and majesty of the unicorn lends itself perfectly to the visual medium of film. There are an extensive number of films that have portrayed the marvelous unicorn. One of the best known is the popular animated film *The Last Unicorn,* adapted from Peter S. Beagle's novel. *The Last Unicorn* featured voiceovers from many acclaimed Hollywood stars of the 1980s. The unicorn's enduring popularity led *The Last Unicorn* to sell millions of copies to the home market.

Nico the Unicorn is a Canadian film that tells the tale of Billy, a physically handicapped boy who has just moved to rural Vermont with his mother Julie. When Billy and Julie visit a local petting zoo, they adopt a pregnant pony with a single horn taped to her forehead. Although the pony itself is not truly a unicorn, her foal is, as it is born with a single horn. Billy names the unicorn Nico, from the letters in the word unicorn. Billy knows that Nico should be kept secret because many people would seek to exploit him. Unfortunately, two disreputable local men learn of Nico's existence and take the unicorn's photograph, selling it to a news reporter in exchange for a large sum of money. To protect Nico from exploitation, Billy runs away from home with him, heading towards a nearby mountain. Upon discovering a portal in the mountain, Billy enters the unicorns' true dimensional home and desires to stay with Nico in this paradise. While taking a drink from a stream, Billy sees his mother's sad face in the water and knows he must leave the unicorns' domain and return home. When Billy returns to his home, a mob of reporters and local residents ask him about Nico, to which Billy replies with a smirk, "What unicorn? Everyone knows unicorns don't exist."

Unico is a series of Japanese animated films from the 1970s and 1980s that feature a baby unicorn named Unico. Unico's special power is his ability to make all creatures happy and carefree. In these films, Unico's extraordinary ability brings him into conflict with the false Gods, who believe they have the exclusive right to control people's feelings. The false Gods decide to banish Unico to the Hill of Oblivion and order the West Wind to carry out their plan, yet the West Wind refuses. Furious at the West Wind for this transgression, the false Gods send the Night Wind to capture both the West Wind and Unico. Upon learning of this nefarious plan, the West Wind saves Unico, transporting him from place to place, allowing Unico to bestow happiness on every being he encounters.

The farcical film *Have Rocket, Will Travel*, released in 1959, has the comedic legends The Three Stooges working as janitors at a space center. Through a series of zany mishaps, The Three Stooges accidentally set off for the planet Venus. Upon reaching Venus, the Stooges encounter a giant firebreathing tarantula, an alien computer, and an extremely talkative unicorn; naturally, mayhem develops.

Director Ridley Scott's fantasy film *Legend* has two unicorns that serve as guardians of the Power of Light, keeping the world warm and abundant. To free himself and seize the light, the Lord of Darkness orders his minions to kill the unicorns and bring their horns to him. Sadly, one of the unicorns succumbs to the Lord of Darkness' evil plot, plunging the world into an impromptu winter. Fortunately, the remaining unicorn and its friends expel the Lord of Darkness into the void, preventing the world from falling into an endless night devoid of light. These films are but a few examples of the many appearances the unicorn has made on the silver screen.

The Unicorn in Music

Across all genres, musicians and songwriters have found a wealth of inspiration from the magical mythical unicorn. World famous singer, songwriter, and actress Lady Gaga has a song titled *Highway Unicorn (Road to Love)* on her album *Born This Way*. In this song, Lady Gaga utilizes the unicorn symbolically. She implores her listeners to have the courage to choose the path of love at all times, regardless of any difficulties that doing so may bring.

The Unicorns were a Canadian pop-rock band. One of their best-known songs is *I Was Born (A Unicorn)*. The song's lyrics state that the unicorn was separated from other animals during the great flood referred to in various spiritual traditions.

American rapper 2 Chainz's song *Black Unicorn* is about being true to yourself, overcoming adversity, and recognizing love. To transmit the song's messages, 2 Chainz metaphorically draws on the unicorn.

American singer Kenny Loggins released *Return to Pooh Corner*, an album of children's songs. *The Last Unicorn*, one of the songs on *Return to Pooh Corner*, was a cover of Jimmy Webb's song in the film *The Last Unicorn*. This song relates how when all life as we know it comes to its end, the unicorn will survive, a nod to the unicorn's incredible transitional ability.

Another song on the soundtrack of *The Last Unicorn*, composed and arranged by Jimmy Webb, is *In The Sea*. This song ponders the question of where the elusive and mysterious unicorn resides. Webb implies that one may connect with the unicorn by being attentive to the natural world.

Power pop musician Parry Gripp's song *Space Unicorn* takes a whimsical look at the unicorn. In a playful manner, Gripp's lyrics express the love that is the unicorn's fundamental essence.

Just as contemporary musicians regularly draw inspiration from the unicorn, so too did those in other time periods. One German folk song beautifully summarizes the essence of the unicorn:

I stood in the Maytime meadows
By roses circled round,
Where many a fragile blossom
Was bright upon the ground;
And as though the roses called them
And their wild hearts understood,
The little birds were singing
In the shadows of the wood.

The nightingale among them
Sang sweet and loud and long,
Until a greater voice than hers
Rang out above her song;
For suddenly, between the crags,
Along the narrow vale,
The echoes of a hunting horn
Came clear upon the gale.

The hunter stood beside me
Who blew that mighty horn;
I saw that he was hunting
The gentle unicorn—
But the unicorn is noble,
He knows his gentle birth,
He knows that God has chosen him
Above all beasts of earth.

The Unicorn is noble;

He keeps him safe and high
Upon a narrow path and steep
Climbing to the sky;
And there no man can take him,
He scorns the hunter's gun,
And only a virgin's magic power
Shall tame his haughty heart.

What would be now the state of us
But for this Unicorn,
And what would be the fate of us,
Poor sinners, lost, forlorn?
Oh, may He lead us on and up,
Unworthy though we be,
Into His Father's kingdom,
To dwell eternally!

The unicorn has been a source of wonderment for numerous instrumental musicians. English electronic musician Kieran Hebden, better known as Four Tet, mirrors the ethereal nature of the unicorn in his instrumental entitled *Unicorn*. Heavy metal rockers The Sword draw influence from the unicorn in an instrumental entitled *Unicorn Farm*. These are only a few examples of the many songs from around the world inspired by the magical mythical unicorn.

The Unicorn in Astronomy and the Zodiac

A long time ago, when the Earth was green
There was more kinds of animals than you've ever seen
They'd run around free while the Earth was being born
And the loveliest of all was the unicorn.
– Shel Silverstein, *The Unicorn*

The Monoceros Constellation

In the northern sky, on the Milky Way's celestial equator, lies Monoceros, a constellation named after the magical mythical unicorn. The constellation was first introduced as

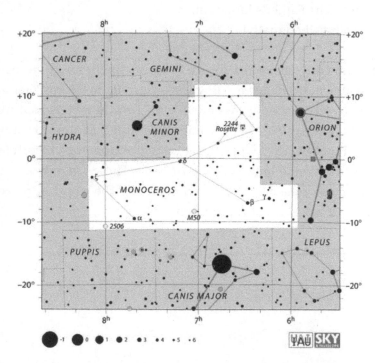

21 – Detailed constellation map of Monoceros from the
International Astronomical Union and *Sky & Telescope* magazine.

Monoceros Unicornis in 1612 on a star map produced by Dutch cartographer and clergyman Petrus Plancius. Plancius had learned of Monoceros from the observations of 17th century Dutch navigators who had begun to chart parts of the sky. It has been suggested that Plancius named the constellation Monoceros either because of the depiction of the unicorn in the Hebrew scriptures or for its resemblance to a scene from *The Hunt of the Unicorn* tapestries. Monoceros is surrounded by Canis Major and Canis Minor, just as the unicorn was surrounded by hunting dogs in *The Hunt of the Unicorn* tapestries, and the nearby constellations of Orion, shaped like the hunter, and Eridanus, shaped like a river, further align with the scenes from the tapestries.

Monoceros has many remarkable celestial features. The unicorn's constellation is famed for having the two most massive stars yet discovered. These stars, known collectively as Plaskett's Star, are believed to be about 55 times the size of our Sun and revolve around one another. They are located at the head of the unicorn in the constellation. In early 2002,

22 – The Constellations of Monoceros, Canis Major, and Canis Minor from a 1729 edition of *Atlas Coelestis*, by John Flamsteed, the first Astronomer Royal.

one of the stars of Monoceros briefly became the Milky Way's most luminous star before evolving into a supergiant that produces light echoes. Additionally, Monoceros is known for the Rosette Nebula, glowing gas shaped in the form of a wreath accompanied by embedded stars.

Although Petrus Plancius is often credited as Monoceros' founder, there is evidence that the constellation had been discovered by the ancient Persians. 17th century French scholar Joseph Justus Scaliger claimed that he had found a reference to the constellation on a Persian sphere from antiquity. Truly, the origins of the discovery of Monoceros are shrouded in mystery.

The Glastonbury Zodiac

The town of Glastonbury in Somerset, England is the home of some of the most sacred esoteric sites and traditions in the world. Once thought of as the mythic Avalon, Glastonbury is believed to be the home of Camelot and the legendary Knights of the Round Table, the land where Merlin the magician trained the young Arthur for his kingship, and the place where Jesus' uncle Joseph of Arimathea brought Jesus to study with the Druids in his formative years and later brought the Holy Grail after Jesus Christ's crucifixion. In this mystical part of England, the unicorn can be seen from above.

England's breathtaking Glastonbury Zodiac are accurate pictorial depictions in the landscape of the twelve signs of the zodiac that are only visible from the air. In the Glastonbury Zodiac, the sign of Capricorn is represented by the unicorn. This link between the unicorn and Capricorn is appropriate, as both are transformational in their essence. In the Northern Hemisphere, the sign of Capricorn ushers in the Winter Solstice. Mary Caine of England, a leading figure in the study of the arcane, explained in her book *The Glastonbury Zodiac* that, "Earthy Capricorn is still the grave of the dying year.

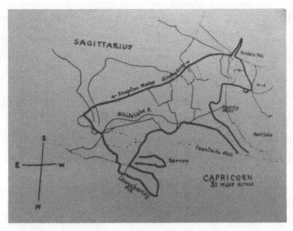

23 – Overhead view of Capricorn from Mary Caine's book *The Glastonbury Zodiac: Key to the Mysteries of Britain.*

His horn is the Cornucopia, where seeds of the coming spring were stored." As Caine explained, the time of Capricorn in late December is often viewed as a desolate period; however, Capricorn presents the Winter Solstice, which brings forth the end of darkness and the return of light. While little bursts forth until spring, the efforts put forth by Capricorn are critical to the yearly cycle of death and rebirth. Caine further explained that, "In the Dionysian Mysteries the goat-stag [Capricorn] symbolized man's immortality, its spiral-patterned horn, like the unicorn's, figuring forth the recurring round of Zodiac lives by which man slowly ascends, as on a spiral stairway, to ever-heightening awareness." It can be said that the horn of Capricorn, like that of the unicorn with which Capricorn represents, is meant to esoterically symbolize spiritual initiation into states of higher vibration through the opening of the all-seeing eye.

The Unicorn and the Moon

There is an extensive tradition that connects the unicorn to the Moon. Ptolemy, an acclaimed astronomer, astrologer, and author of ancient Greece, suggested that the Moon, like the unicorn and its horn, had powerful healing properties. Various myths have connected the unicorn to lunar energy. The unicorn is sometimes placed in rivalry and other times in alliance with the lion, a solar figure. The supposed opposition of the unicorn and the lion towards each other, if viewed from the lens of their symbolizing the Moon and Sun, may be understood as a creative retelling of the daily cycles of these two celestial bodies. Night and day, like the unicorn and the lion, are interconnected. Perhaps the myths of the unicorn and lion's rivalry serve a deeper purpose. Is it possible that these celestial legends are metaphors intended to symbolize the esoteric principle of as above so below, and show people that opposites must be united and balanced before peace, harmony, and higher consciousness can emerge?

The Unicorn's Horn

*The Unicorn... the beautiful white horse with the magical horn
that heals.*
– Author Unknown

There are a multiplicity of traditions and legends about the
unicorn's horn within the history and mythology of the world,
though its use was perhaps most recorded in medieval Europe,
where the horn was known as the alicorn. The unicorn's horn
has been revered by people across the globe for a wide variety
of reasons, not the least of which is its profound ability to
heal. No feature of the unicorn has been as closely associated
with healing as its majestic spiraled horn. The horn's power
to heal and transform has long been a source of wonder, with
these attributes coming from its connection to the third eye,
or expanded consciousness. The unicorn's horn can heal not
only the body, but also the mind and heart, bringing one into
a balanced state.

The Alicorn and European Royalty
Around the beginning of the 13th century, the alicorn started
to become a major part of European culture. By that time,
Asian traditions about the unicorn's amazing ability to
purify poisoned waters for other animals had begun to filter

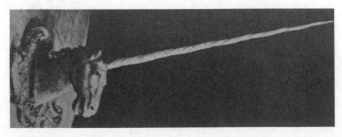

24 – Sign from an apothecary in Rottenbuch, Germany, circa 1750.

into Europe. Commonly known as the water-conning story, these tales revolved around how animals would wait for the unicorn to dip its horn into poisoned water to eliminate all of the maladies that would come from drinking or bathing in the water. Many travelers from Europe who visited other parts of the globe were able to learn about and witness the healing properties of the unicorn's horn. After Europeans heard these incredible stories that the travelers brought back with them, they became curious about the power of the alicorn to heal and detect poisons. Europeans began to investigate and later believe in the alicorn's medicinal attributes.

Until the 16th century, alicorns were purchased and used exclusively by Europe's wealthiest individuals. Many European kings and queens owned full intact alicorns, including King Edward I of England, King Charles VI of France, King Henry II of France, King Philip II of Spain (who was said to have acquired twelve alicorns), Mary, Queen of Scots, King Francis I of France, Queen Elizabeth I of England, and numerous other royal figures. King Frederick III of Denmark even chose to have his throne made entirely of alicorns. Some churches, including St. Denis in Paris and St. Mark's in Venice, also owned alicorns, displaying them as sacred objects that were held in awe by the people. To these powerful individuals and institutions, owning an alicorn signified wealth and prestige. However, such value came at a steep price. One such example is in 1560, when German merchants sold the Pope an alicorn for 90,000 scudi, an exorbitant sum for the time.

During Europe's Middle Ages, poisoning became common-place as a tactic performed to eliminate political rivals. The fear that one may sit down for a meal or beverage and meet their demise at the hands of a frustrated subject, an ambitious relative, or a ruthless political opponent weighed on the minds of European royalty. Fortunately, the introduction of the alicorn presented a solution; its magic could determine whether food and drink had been poisoned. The alicorn would sweat in the presence of poison. European royalty believed that when dipped into a tainted item, the alicorn would neutralize all effects of the harmful substance. Because of these properties as an antidote, the magical alicorn became invaluable to European dignitaries, who eagerly sought to purchase alicorns to protect themselves and their families.

Unfortunately, there have always been individuals who seek to profit via exploitation. In Europe, a fraudulent market developed soon after the introduction of the alicorn. Swindlers made a lucrative trade out of producing and selling fake horns. David de Pomis, a 16th century Italian Jewish physician, wrote that, "There is very little of the true horn to be found, most of that which is sold being either stag's horn, or elephant's tusk." Other items sold in place of the true unicorn horn included bull horns, goat horns, rhinoceros horns, artificially-straightened walrus tusks, fossil bones, dog bones, petrified wood, stalactites, and many other substances. Fake horns regularly made their way to wealthy individuals, perhaps most notably in the case of King James I of England and Scotland. After King James purchased what he believed was an alicorn, he chose to test it on a servant. Regrettably for the servant, his King had been deceived.

The Alicorn as a European Panacea

While owning an entire alicorn remained a privilege of the elite, in the 16th century, powders and chunks of alicorn started to be sold widely in apothecary shops throughout Europe. This change led to use of the alicorn being embraced by many Europeans, regardless of whether they were rich or poor. People of all backgrounds utilized the alicorn to combat scurvy, ulcers, dropsy, gout, consumption, distillations, coughs, heart palpitations, fainting, convulsions, king's evil, rickets, melancholy, sadness, green sickness, obstructions, impotence, frigidity, fever, the plague, cramps, epilepsy, leprosy, aging, colic, rabies, poison – even raising the dead. The use of alicorn was so common that the Apothecaries Society of London, founded in 1617, chose to place unicorns on their coat of arms in a symbolic nod to the healing powers of the unicorn. At the time, it was even a common sight to see an alicorn chained to an apothecary's counter to signify that this was a place of healing. Remarkably, some of these wondrous alicorns still survive into the present, including one at the White Unicorn pharmacy in Klatovy, Czech Republic, a UNESCO World Heritage Site.

The Scientific Wars

For centuries, the unicorn's existence was a matter of fact to most. Author Margoulies wrote in the 9th century that, "It is universally held that the unicorn is a supernatural being and an auspicious omen; so say the odes, the annals, the biographies of worthies, and other texts whose authority is unimpeachable. Even village women and children know the unicorn is a lucky sign." Yet in 1566, after over a millennium of belief in the unicorn and its horn throughout Europe, an Italian physician named Andrea Marini penned a widely-read book that erroneously scoffed at the notion that the alicorn had the power to heal. His controversial premise defied beliefs held by royalty, clergy, and the average European of the time.

In the wake of Marini's work, Don Francesco Medici, a faithful believer in the unicorn and member of one of Italy's most prominent families, feared what might result from a weakened popular belief in the unicorn. Andrea Bacci, an author who received the patronage of Medici, was commissioned to write a passionate defense of the unicorn and the curative properties of its horn. Bacci's book presented scientific evidence from an experiment performed by the Cardinal of Trent. The Cardinal gave arsenic to two pigeons. Afterwards, only one of the pigeons was fed alicorn powder. The pigeon that received the alicorn powder survived, whereas the other pigeon died in less than two hours. Bacci's example was only one of the many proofs presented at the time to defend the alicorn's use as a medical treatment. During the 16th century, a variety of experiments were performed in many European countries to study the alicorn's ability to heal. Whether scientists tested the power of the alicorn on scorpions, spiders, or through the many other methods that they utilized, the results were consistent – the alicorn was found to have genuine healing properties.

Unfortunately, those affected by Marini's writings became skeptical of the alicorn's powers and started to exert a major influence on some segments of European society. The scientific community was the first to be affected, with many physicians and scientists incorrectly claiming that the alicorn held no power to heal. Some physicians and scientists were even doubtful of the unicorn's existence altogether, a position that would have been unthinkable to publicly hold in prior centuries. In time, the cynicism of many intellectual leaders spread to the European aristocracy, and eventually to many other Europeans.

The Fall of the European Market

Because of the controversy that came from the negative writings of many intellectuals, sales of alicorns began to decline in Europe. Clever European merchants now had to resort to a different approach to make money from alicorn sales. Many of these merchants began to turn to markets outside of Europe. According to Odell Shepard in *The Lore of the Unicorn*, attempts to sell the alicorn in Russia, Turkey, and the Near East were not profitable. However, efforts to sell the unicorn's horn in China and Japan were far more lucrative. The people of these lands were familiar with the horn's many medicinal benefits, and had utilized the horn for millennia, having a long history of purchasing unicorn horn from Indian, Middle Eastern, Ethiopian, and Southeast Asian traders.

The Narwhal

For centuries, Denmark had a monopoly on the sale of artificial unicorn horns throughout Europe. Being a seafaring people, many Danes would voyage north to the Arctic, where they secured the tusks of the narwhal, an aquatic mammal that was rarely seen south of the Danish territory of Greenland. The male narwhal has a distinctive feature – a singular ivory horn, which some refer to as a tusk, that juts out of its jaw, above its lips, and grows in a spiral for up to eight feet. From as early as the year 1126, enterprising Danes developed a lucrative trade selling the similar-looking narwhal's tusk as the alicorn, both in Denmark and across the Mediterranean and Black Sea areas.

Until recent centuries the narwhal was unfamiliar to mainland Europeans. This fact allowed the Danes to sell narwhal tusks as alicorns for more than five centuries. When knowledge of the narwhal finally began to emerge, some Europeans were convinced that it was a unicorn of the seas. Those who asserted that the narwhal was an aquatic unicorn often believed that its horn-like tusk had the same beneficial properties as the alicorn. Their reasoning was that if the narwhal were a sea-based unicorn, then it must have all the same attributes. Others contended that the narwhal was not a unicorn at all, and therefore its tusk was ineffective against illnesses. Despite the arguments of those who doubted the healing qualities of the narwhal's tusk, most Europeans believed in the curative properties of both the alicorn and the tusk of the narwhal. Even today, the legacy of the power of the narwhal's tusk remains, as it continues to be sold throughout the world for a wide variety of purposes.

The Unicorn and the Third Eye

Nothing is more magical... As long as they roam the Earth, evil cannot harm the pure of heart.
– Reference to the unicorn from the movie *Legend*

The Unicorn and Humanity's Ascension

The third eye, also referred to as the pineal gland and all-seeing eye, is associated with intuition, clairvoyance, and precognition. Manly P. Hall, founder of the esteemed Philosophical Research Society, wrote that, "The single horn of the unicorn may represent the pineal gland, or third eye, which is the spiritual cognition center in the brain." As Hall attested, the unicorn's horn is a manifestation of the third eye. Should one desire to find the secret associated with humankind's pending transformation and ascension, it may be essential to look to the unicorn. Classicist Robert Graves suggested that the word unicorn means "find the secret." It is possible that the secret which Graves alluded to might be the transcendent unicorn's connection to humanity's shift into higher dimensional realities.

The Third Eye in Spirituality

Throughout time and across cultures, great spiritual teachers, seers, astrologers, healers, clairvoyants, and channelers have drawn on the elevated consciousness brought forth through the third eye. In the spiritual traditions of Hinduism and Jainism, the third eye is given explicit recognition through the practice of decorating women's foreheads with a bindi, or red dot, at the third eye chakra energy center. This practice is extensive throughout India, Pakistan, Bangladesh, Nepal, Sri Lanka, and amongst Hindus in Bali and Java. Within Hinduism, Jainism, Buddhism, and other spiritual traditions, the third eye is understood as the beginning point and is symbolic of complete cosmic unification. When the third eye chakra is activated, transcendence into higher dimensional vibrations can be achieved.

A Look Into the Future?

Despite the apparent discord that marks humankind's current state, referred to as the Kali Yuga or Iron Age, this cyclical age is coming to its conclusion. According to the Mayan calendar, this event has already transpired in 2012. The Satya Yuga or Golden Age is returning, shifting dimensions and bringing forth incredible spiritual perceptions and knowledge that are opening humanity's collective third eye, a process which the multidimensional unicorn symbolizes. *The Codex Unicornis* reminds us that the unicorn points the way and guards the gate into this higher vibrational reality.

The Unicorn in Alchemy and the Mystery Schools

Think of the Unicorn, that curious symbol of retirement from the world.

– Edward Carpenter, "Tradition, Convention, and the Gods"

The Mystery Schools

Mystery Schools, originally centered in ancient Egypt, have been centers of spiritual teachings of esoteric knowledge throughout time. Initiates of these schools are taught the myriad secrets of spiritual and esoteric traditions. One of the Mystery Schools' secret teachings is alchemy's connection to the unicorn. Manly P. Hall, an enlightened and respected philosopher and esotericist of the 20th century, explained in *The Secret Teachings of All Ages* that, "The unicorn was adopted by the Mysteries as a symbol of the illumined spiritual nature of the initiate, the horn with which it defends itself being the flaming sword of the spiritual doctrine against, which nothing can prevail." If the essence of Hall's words are properly understood, then alchemy can help us to understand the symbolism of the unicorn.

The Unicorn in the Alchemical Process

The Book of Lambspring, written in the 16th century, is one of many texts thought to be associated with the Mystery Schools. The book features an illustration of a unicorn and a deer in a wooded area. Next to the picture is a description: "The Sages say truly that two animals are in this forest: One glorious, beautiful, and swift, a great and strong deer; the other a unicorn. If we apply the parable of our art [alchemy], we shall call the forest the body. The unicorn will be the spirit at all times. The deer desires no other name but that of the soul. He that knows how to tame and master them by art, to couple them together, and to lead them in and out of the form, may justly be called a Master." To put this passage another way, the unicorn is the essence of the human spirit. All living things aim to know their inner divinity and higher purpose. Through striving to be like the unicorn, in tune with our spiritual natures, we can gain knowledge and transcend our perceived reality.

One of the many symbolic representations of the unicorn's magical horn in the esoteric Mysteries was its serving as a symbol for Osiris, one the foremost gods of ancient Egypt. Osiris was murdered at the hands of Seth, but became reborn through the powers of spirituality and magic. From this basis in Egyptian tradition, Osiris has been associated with the subconscious, or underworld, and symbolized the process of rebirth and regeneration. The unicorn horn's connection to Osiris is appropriate, as one of the spiritual secrets of the Mystery Schools is the symbolic association between the unicorn and rebirth, resurrection, and the process of ascension.

The Essence of Alchemy

Much like the unicorn, alchemy is also noted for its transformative nature. On the surface, this takes the form of turning metals into gold, although the practice is not intended to be a quest for riches or glory. The gold of the alchemist represents an inward change to purity and a higher consciousness. The successful alchemist is said to be able to transcend the perceived fixed rules of matter. In so doing, it is believed that the alchemist ascends closer to the Universal Mind, much like the unicorn.

It has been suggested that although many alchemists spent their entire lives engaged in the practice, few realized alchemy's end goal – the creation of the Philosopher's Stone.

An alchemist who discovers the metaphorical Philosopher's Stone is said to reach immortality. For alchemists, finding the Philosopher's Stone is known as the Magnum Opus, or Great Work. Once the Magnum Opus is achieved, the alchemist's character is thought to mirror that of the unicorn – transformed, enlightened, and transcendent.

Conclusion

"The unicorn," she said, "was a marvelous beast, shining with honor, wisdom and strength. Just to see him strengthened the soul."
– Megan Lindholm, "The Unicorn in the Maze"

The Unicorn Today

The magical mythical unicorn is revealing the fullness of its essence to humanity. The Golden Age is once again ushering in dimensional shifts that are affecting the Earth and leading humanity towards transformation, awakening, and higher consciousness. As each day draws this wonderful new era closer and closer, the unicorn's activity is becoming ever more prevalent. In our chaotic world, one where separation instead of unity has become the norm, the unicorn points the way to the essence of spirit – the truth, purity, and love that have purposely been subjugated in the name of divisiveness and dehumanizing technological progress. The unicorn in its reemergence is communicating with humanity, informing us that we must recognize the false programming that has been thrust upon us and choose to return to the innocence, beauty, and purpose to which we were all born. When we wake up from illusion, we shall meet the unicorn and love shall reign. Today, everywhere we seem to look there is a unicorn to remind us of this certainty. The unicorn is everywhere: toys, coloring books, greeting cards, costumes, literature, film, media, personal encounters, language, etc. The unicorn's reemergence into the global consciousness is a symbolic clue of what is forthcoming: the lighting of the flame of our higher consciousness, with the unicorn leading humankind to ascension.

The Unicorn and the Upcoming Golden Age

Humanity is awakening from its slumber. A rapidly increasing amount of people each day are becoming aware of the cosmic realities that govern life on our planet and the responsibility that we all have to work towards the greatest good. In response to this immense global shift in consciousness, unicorns are appearing more frequently.

In *The Codex Unicornis*, Master Magnalucius divulged that the unicorn is the guardian of the light. Light is the opposite of darkness and ignorance. Light signifies one's consciousness, the understanding that all is one. Light is awareness. Once humanity crosses the threshold and ascends into the light, it will move across the dimensions into a new Golden Age where peace, love, and enlightenment triumph, and darkness holds no sway. When this breakthrough occurs, it will be the end of the third dimension as it is currently understood.

The universal unicorn, whether called karkadann, as the Arabs called it, ki-lin as the Chinese called it, kau maha as the Maoris called it, or by any other name, is beginning to share itself more visibly with humanity in this era of rapid change. According to *The Codex Unicornis*, when the time is right, it is said that the unicorn will reveal the mysterious Three Secret Sayings. Upon these revelations from the unicorn, this current age will reach its conclusion and a new Golden Age shall begin.

> *"Well, now that we have seen each other," said the unicorn, "if you'll believe in me, I'll believe in you."*
> – Lewis Carroll, *Through the Looking-Glass*

The Unicorn and Your Destiny

The unicorn is the most magical of all animals. It can shift between our visible world and other worlds beyond the five senses. If you are open to its guidance, the unicorn can show

25 – Alice with the unicorn and lion from Lewis Carroll's *Alice's Adventures in Wonderland*.

you that your life has incredible possibilities. You can become the best version of yourself and live the life which you desire. The unicorn wants to help you transform yourself and is available to help you. When you call out for the unicorn's help, know that it will appear before you. The unicorn can appear in your dreams, in symbolism, or in any number of ways for it knows no boundaries.

The unicorn wants to challenge you to become that best version of yourself. Fear and doubt can destroy all of the wonder of life. The unicorn offers you a choice. Do you want to stay where you are, stuck in limitations, or will you have the courage and wisdom to believe that more is possible, that your dreams can be achieved, and that you can become the most authentic version of yourself? If you can hear what the unicorn is communicating to you, then you can realize that all boundaries are illusions and the truth is that anything that you can imagine is possible to manifest.

The magic that the unicorn represents comes from its horn, which can not only heal and balance you, but also teaches the mystery of how to achieve what we are destined for, that in the direction and application of our thoughts we can complete any objective. Truly, you can make your dreams a reality. Are you ready to shift your perspective? Are you ready to challenge conventional wisdom? Then you can shed the old hurts and pain and frustration and embrace a new world, one where fear is nothing but an illusion. In business, there's a term called "the unicorn effect" that indicates that a business has risen in success so quickly it mimics the magic of the unicorn. You too can have your own personal unicorn effect if you are open to shedding your old ways and embracing a better and truer path. Do you want to meet the unicorn and step into your new life?

Works Cited

Aelian. *On the Characteristics of Animals*. Edited and translated by AF Scholfield. Heinemann, 1958.

Alexander, Skye. *Unicorns: The Myths, Legends, & Lore*. Adams Media, 2015.

America and Jimmy Webb. "Where Do Unicorns Go?" *The Last Unicorn*, EMI Import, 1994.

Aristotle. *History of Animals*. Edited and translated by Richard Cresswell. George Bell and Sons, 1883.

The Atharvaveda. Translated by Devi Chand, 2002 edition. Munshiram, 1997.

Auden, WH. *Collected Poems*. Edited by Edward Mendelson. Random House, 1976.

Beagle, Peter S. *The Last Unicorn*. Viking Press, 1968.

Beer, Rüdiger Robert. *Unicorn: Myth and Reality*. Mason/ Charter, 1977.

Borges, Jorge Luis, and Peter Sis. *The Book of Imaginary Beings*. Translated by Andrew Hurley. Penguin Classics, 2006.

Bradley, Josephine. *In Pursuit of the Unicorn*. Pomegranate Art Books, 1980.

Brothers Grimm. *The Brave Little Tailor*. Amazon Digital Services LLC, 2017.

Caine, Mary. *The Glastonbury Giants*. Mary Caine, 1976.

Caine, Mary. *The Glastonbury Zodiac: Key to the Mysteries of Britain*. Mary Caine, 1978.

Carroll, Lewis. *Alice's Adventures in Wonderland & Through the Looking-Glass*. Bantam Classics, 1984.

Cavendish, Richard. *Man, Myth & Magic: An Illustrated Encyclopedia of the Supernatural*. Marshall Cavendish Corp., 1970.

Chatwin, Bruce. *In Patagonia*. Penguin Classics, 2003.

Clark, Anne. *Beasts and Bawdy*. Taplinger Pub. Co., 1975.

Contadini, Anna. "A Bestiary Tale: Text and Image of the Unicorn in the Kitāb Na't Al-Hayawān." *Muqarnas*, vol. 20, 2003, pp. 17–33.

Cooper, Diana. *The Wonder of Unicorns*. Findhorn Press, 2008.

Cooper, JC. *An Illustrated Encyclopedia of Traditional Symbols*. New edition, Thames & Hudson, 1987.

d'Allemagne, Henry-René. *Du Khorassan au Pays Des Backhtiaris, Trois Mois de Voyage En Perse*. Hachette Livre – BNF, 2018.

Dankoff, Robert. "Kāšġarī on the Beliefs and Superstitions of the Turks." *Journal of the American Oriental Society*, vol. 95, no. 1, Jan.-Mar. 1975, pp. 68–80.

Delphinas, Nicholas Barnaud. *The Book of Lambspring*. Theophania Publishing, 2011.

de Vries, Ad. *Dictionary of Symbols and Imagery*. 2nd edition, North-Holland Pub. Co., 1974.

Ettinghausen, Richard. *The Unicorn: Studies in Muslim Iconography*. Smithsonian Institution, 1950.

The Fantastic Adventures of Unico. Directed by Toshio Hirata and Osamu Tezuka, performances by Katsue Miwa, Ryouko Kitamiya, and Kazuko Sugiyama, Sanrio Communications, 1981.

Four Tet. "Unicorn." Text Records, 2017. *Spotify*.

Fox-Davies, Arthur Charles. *A Complete Guide to Heraldry*. Bonanza Books, 1978.

Freeman, Margaret B. *The Unicorn Tapestries*. Metropolitan Museum of Art, 1974.

Funk & Wagnall's Standard Dictionary of Folklore, Mythology and Legend. Edited by Maria Leach. Harper & Row, 1972.

Gaiman, Neil, and Charles Vess. *Stardust*. Vertigo/DC Comics, 1998.

Gould, Charles. *Mythical Monsters, Cryptozoology: A Study on the Dragon, Unicorn, Phoenix and Other Species*. Forgotten Books, 2007.

Green, Michael. *De Historia et Veritate Unicornis: On the History and Truth of the Unicorn*. Running Press Book Publishers, 1983.

Gripp, Parry. "Space Unicorn." Parry Gripp, 2011. *Spotify*.

Haggard, Howard W. *Devils, Drugs, and Doctors: The Story of the Science of Healing from Medicine-Man to Doctor*. Harper & Brothers, 1929.

Hall, Manly P. *The Secret Teachings of All Ages: An Encyclopedic Outline of Masonic, Hermetic, Qabbalistic and Rosicrucian Symbolical Philosophy*. CreateSpace Independent Publishing Platform, 2011.

Hastings' Dictionary of the Bible. Edited by James Hastings. Reprint edition, Baker Books, 1994.

Hathaway, Nancy. *The Unicorn*. Penguin Books, 1982.

Have Rocket, Will Travel. Directed by David Lowell Rich, performances by Moe Howard, Larry Fine, Joe De Rita, Jerome Cowan, and Anna-Lisa, SPE, 1959.

The Holy Bible. Authorized King James Version, Biblica.

The Holy Qur'an. Translated by Abdullah Yusuf Ali. 5th edition, Wordsworth Editions, Ltd., 2001.

Hussein Ali, Zahra A. "The Aesthetics of Dissonance: Echoes of Nietzsche and Yeats in Tawfiq Sayigh's Poetry." *Journal of Arabic Literature*, vol. 30, no. 1, 1999, pp. 1–54.

The I Ching. Translated by Richard Wilhelm and Cary F. Baynes. 3rd edition, Princeton University Press, 1967.

Johnsgard, Paul, and Karin Johnsgard. *Dragons and Unicorns: A Natural History*. Reprint edition, St. Martin's Griffin, 1992.

Jung, CG. *Psychology and Alchemy*. Translated by RFC Hull. Pantheon Books, 1953.

Lady Gaga. "Highway Unicorn (Road to Love)." Interscope, 2011. *Spotify*.

The Last Unicorn. Directed by Arthur Rankin Jr. and Jules Bass, performances by Mia Farrow, Alan Arkin, and Jeff

Bridges, Shout! Factory, 1982.

Legend. Directed by Ridley Scott, performances by Tom Cruise, Mia Sara, and Tim Curry, Universal Pictures, 1986.

Lewinsohn, Richard. *Animals, Men and Myths: An Informative and Entertaining History of Man and the Animals Around Him*. Harper & Brothers, 1954.

Lewis, CS, and Pauline Baynes. *The Last Battle*. Reprint edition, HarperCollins, 2002.

Ley, Willy. "The Fabulous Monoceros." Review of *Studies in Muslim Iconography: The Unicorn*, by Richard Ettinghausen. *The Scientific Monthly*, vol. 72, no. 3, March 1951, p. 198.

Loggins, Kenny. "The Last Unicorn." Sony Music Entertainment, 1994. *Spotify*.

Lum, Peter, and Anne Marie Jauss. *Fabulous Beasts*. First British edition, Farrar, Thames & Hudson, 1952.

Lutz, Cora E. "The American Unicorn." *The Yale University Library Gazette*, vol. 53, no. 3, January 1979, pp. 135–139.

The Mahabharata. Translated by Bibek Debroy. Twenty-first edition, Penguin, 2015.

Majka, Richard. "The Unicorn As Myth and Symbol." *The Rosicrucian Digest*, May 1977, pp. 10–13.

McCaughrean, Geraldine. *Unicorns! Unicorns!* Holiday House, 1997.

McCrindle, JW. *Ancient India as Described by Ktèsias the Knidian: Being a Translation of the Abridcement of His "Indika" by Photios, and of the Fragments of That Work Preserved in Other Writers*. Forgotten Books, 2018.

McInnes, Judy. "Arthurian Material in Angelina Muñiz Huberman's 'La Guerra del Unicornio'." *Hispanic Journal*, vol. 22, no. 1, 2001, pp. 217–225.

Megged, Matti. *The Animal That Never Was: In Search of the Unicorn*. Lumen Books, 1992.

Meinardus, Otto FA. "The Damascus Unicorn Bowl." *Orientalia, NOVA Series*, vol. 64, no. 3, 1995, pp. 223–224.

Muñiz-Huberman, Angelina. *La Guerra del Unicornio*. Artífice Ediciones, 1983.

Mythical and Fabulous Creatures: A Source Book and Research Guide. Edited by Malcolm South. Peter Bedrick Books, 1988.

Nico the Unicorn. Directed by Graeme Campbell, performances by Anne Archer, Elisha Cuthbert, and Maggie Castle, Screen Media Ventures, 1998.

Paludan, Ann. *The Imperial Ming Tombs*. Yale University Press, 1981.

Pedler, Frederick. *The Lion and the Unicorn in Africa: United Africa Company, 1787–1931*. 1st edition, Heinemann Educational Books, 1974.

Physiologus. Edited and translated by Michael J. Curley. University of Chicago Press, 2009.

Poltarnees, Welleran. *A Book of Unicorns*. Star and Elephant Books, 1978.

Radka, Larry Brian. *Historical Evidence for Unicorns*. Einhorn Press, 1995.

The Rig Veda. Edited and translated by Wendy Doniger. Reprinted edition, Penguin Classics, 2005.

Rilke, Rainer Maria. *Sonnets to Orpheus*. Translated by MD Herter Norton, 1st edition. WW Norton & Co., 2006.

Rowling, JK. *Harry Potter and the Sorcerer's Stone*. Scholastic Press, 1998.

Shakespeare, William. *Julius Caesar*. Edited by Barbara A. Mowat and Paul Werstine. Reissue edition, Simon & Schuster, 2004.

Shakespeare, William. *The Tempest*. Edited by Robert Langbaum. Updated edition, Signet, 1998.

Shakespeare, William. *Timon of Athens*. Edited by Karl Klein. Cambridge University Press, 2001.

The Shatapatha Brahmana. Translated by Julius Eggeling. CreateSpace Independent Publishing Platform, 2015.

Shepard, Odell. *The Lore of the Unicorn*. George Allen & Unwin/Houghton Mifflin, 1930.

Silverstein, Shel. "The Unicorn." Nifty Music, Inc., 2011. *Spotify*.

Stetkevych, Jaroslav. "In Search of the Unicorn: The Onager and the Oryx in the Arabic Ode." *Journal of Arabic Literature*, vol. 33, no. 2, 2002, pp. 79–130.

The Sword. "Unicorn Farm." Razor & Tie, 2015. *Spotify*.

Topsell, Edward. *The History of Four-Footed Beasts and Serpents*. Isha Books, 2013.

2 Chainz. Featuring Chrisette Michele and Sunni Patterson. "Black Unicorn." Def Jam Records, 2013. *Spotify*.

The Unicorns. "I Was Born (A Unicorn)." Caterpillar, 2014. *Spotify*.

Valmiki. *The Ramayana*. Translated by Arshia Sattar. Penguin Global, 2010.

Viré, F. "Karkaddan," in *Encyclopaedia of Islam, Second Edition*. Edited by P. Bearman, Th. Bianquis, CE Bosworth, E. van Donzel, WP Heinrichs. Consulted online on 16 December 2017.

Wigoder, Geoffrey, Shalom M. Paul, and Benedict T. Viviano. *Almanac of the Bible*. Macmillan General Reference, 1991.

Williams, Tennessee. *The Glass Menagerie*. New Directions Books, 1999.

Yeats, William Butler. *The Unicorn from the Stars*. 1st edition, CreateSpace Independent Publishing Platform, 2015.

Zelazny, Roger. *The Great Book of Amber*. Avon Eos, 1999.

BOOKS

O-BOOKS

SPIRITUALITY

O is a symbol of the world, of oneness and unity; this eye
represents knowledge and insight. We publish titles on
general spirituality and living a spiritual life. We aim to
inform and help you on your own journey in this life.
If you have enjoyed this book, why not tell other readers by
posting a review on your preferred book site?

Recent bestsellers from O-Books are:

Heart of Tantric Sex
Diana Richardson
Revealing Eastern secrets of deep love and intimacy to
Western couples.
Paperback: 978-1-90381-637-0 ebook: 978-1-84694-637-0

Crystal Prescriptions
The A-Z guide to over 1,200 symptoms and the stones that
heal them
Judy Hall
The first in the popular series of six books, this handy little
guide is packed as tight as a pill-bottle with crystal remedies
for ailments.
Paperback: 978-1-90504-740-6 ebook: 978-1-84694-629-5

Take Me To Truth
Undoing the Ego
Nouk Sanchez, Tomas Vieira
The best-selling step-by-step book on shedding the Ego, using
the teachings of *A Course In Miracles*.
Paperback: 978-1-84694-050-7 ebook: 978-1-84694-654-7

The 7 Myths about Love...Actually!
The journey from your HEAD to the HEART of your SOUL
Mike George
Smashes all the myths about LOVE.
Paperback: 978-1-84694-288-4 ebook: 978-1-84694-682-0

The Holy Spirit's Interpretation of the New Testament

A Course in Understanding and Acceptance

Regina Dawn Akers

Following on from the strength of *A Course In Miracles*, NTI teaches us how to experience the love and oneness of God.

Paperback: 978-1-84694-085-9 ebook: 978-1-78099-083-5

The Message of A Course In Miracles

A translation of the Text in plain language

Elizabeth A. Cronkhite

A translation of *A Course in Miracles* into plain, everyday language for anyone seeking inner peace. The companion volume, *Practicing A Course In Miracles*, offers practical lessons and mentoring.

Paperback: 978-1-84694-319-5 ebook: 978-1-84694-642-4

Rising in Love

My Wild and Crazy Ride to Here and Now, with Amma, the Hugging Saint

Ram Das Batchelder

Rising in Love conveys an author's extraordinary journey of spiritual awakening with the Guru, Amma.

Paperback: 978-1-78279-687-9 ebook: 978-1-78279-686-2

Thinker's Guide to God

Peter Vardy

An introduction to key issues in the philosophy of religion.

Paperback: 978-1-90381-622-6

Your Simple Path
Find Happiness in every step
Ian Tucker
A guide to helping us reconnect with what is really important
in our lives.
Paperback: 978-1-78279-349-6 ebook: 978-1-78279-348-9

365 Days of Wisdom
Daily Messages To Inspire You Through The Year
Dadi Janki
Daily messages which cool the mind, warm the heart and
guide you along your journey.
Paperback: 978-1-84694-863-3 ebook: 978-1-84694-864-0

Body of Wisdom
Women's Spiritual Power and How it Serves
Hilary Hart
Bringing together the dreams and experiences of women
across the world with today's most visionary spiritual
teachers.
Paperback: 978-1-78099-696-7 ebook: 978-1-78099-695-0

Dying to Be Free
From Enforced Secrecy to Near Death to True Transformation
Hannah Robinson
After an unexpected accident and near-death experience,
Hannah Robinson found herself radically transforming her
life, while a remarkable new insight altered her relationship
with her father, a practising Catholic priest.
Paperback: 978-1-78535-254-6 ebook: 978-1-78535-255-3

The Ecology of the Soul
A Manual of Peace, Power and Personal Growth for Real
People in the Real World
Aidan Walker
Balance your own inner Ecology of the Soul to regain your
natural state of peace, power and wellbeing.
Paperback: 978-1-78279-850-7 ebook: 978-1-78279-849-1

Not I, Not other than I
The Life and Teachings of Russel Williams
Steve Taylor, Russel Williams
The miraculous life and inspiring teachings of one of the
World's greatest living Sages.
Paperback: 978-1-78279-729-6 ebook: 978-1-78279-728-9

On the Other Side of Love
A woman's unconventional journey towards wisdom
Muriel Maufroy
When life has lost all meaning, what do you do?
Paperback: 978-1-78535-281-2 ebook: 978-1-78535-282-9

Practicing A Course In Miracles
A translation of the Workbook in plain language, with
mentor's notes
Elizabeth A. Cronkhite
The practical second and third volumes of The Plain-Language
A Course In Miracles.
Paperback: 978-1-84694-403-1 ebook: 978-1-78099-072-9

Quantum Bliss
The Quantum Mechanics of Happiness, Abundance, and
Health
George S. Mentz
Quantum Bliss is the breakthrough summary of success and
spirituality secrets that customers have been waiting for.
Paperback: 978-1-78535-203-4 ebook: 978-1-78535-204-1

The Upside Down Mountain
Mags MacKean
A must-read for anyone weary of chasing success and
happiness – one woman's inspirational journey swapping the
uphill slog for the downhill slope.
Paperback: 978-1-78535-171-6 ebook: 978-1-78535-172-3

Your Personal Tuning Fork
The Endocrine System
Deborah Bates
Discover your body's health secret, the endocrine system, and
'twang' your way to sustainable health!
Paperback: 978-1-84694-503-8 ebook: 978-1-78099-697-4

Readers of ebooks can buy or view any of these bestsellers by
clicking on the live link in the title. Most titles are published
in paperback and as an ebook. Paperbacks are available in
traditional bookshops. Both print and ebook formats are
available online.

Find more titles and sign up to our readers' newsletter at
http://www.johnhuntpublishing.com/mind-body-spirit

Follow us on Facebook at https://www.facebook.com/OBooks/
and Twitter at https://twitter.com/obooks